WHEN KIDS GET INTO TROUBLE

For H.R.

This book is dedicated to the parents of children who get in trouble — for their courage, endurance and faith.

WHEN KIDS GET INTO TROUBLE

A GUIDE FOR PARENTS, TEACHERS AND PROFESSIONALS

PRISCILLA PLATT, LL.B.

Ministry of Education, Ontario
Information Centre, 13th Floor,
Mowat Block, Queen's Park,
Toronto, Ont.   M7A 1L2

Copyright © 1987 by Priscilla Platt

All rights reserved. No part of this publication may be reproduced or transmitted in any form or by any means, electronic or mechanical, including photocopy, recording, or any information storage and retrieval system, without permission in writing from the publisher.

First published in 1987 by
Stoddart Publishing Co. Limited
34 Lesmill Road
Toronto, Canada
M3B 2T6

Canadian Cataloguing in Publication Data

Platt, Priscilla
   When kids get into trouble

Includes text of Young Offenders Act.
ISBN 0-7737-5104-1

1. Children — Legal status, laws, etc. 2. Juvenile delinquents — Canada. 3. Canada. Young Offenders Act. I. Canada. Young Offenders Act. II. Title.

KE512.P53 1987   345.71'03   C86-094939-7

Cover design: Brant Cowie/Artplus
Cover illustration: David Craig

Printed in Canada

Contents

Foreword by His Honour Judge Joseph C.M. James	7
Acknowledgments	8
Introduction	9

Chapter One: The *Young Offenders Act* and You   13
The basic differences between the *Young Offenders Act*
  and the *Juvenile Delinquents Act*   13
  1. To what offences and to whom does this Act apply?   13
  2. Sentencing   14
  3. Opening court and enlarging appeal rights   15
What is the philosophy of the Act?   15
Are youth courts criminal courts or
  child protection courts?   16

Chapter Two: The Role of the Police   19
Before a decision to lay a charge has been made   19
  1. The duty to investigate   19
  2. Police discretion   19
After a decision to lay a charge has been made   20
  1. Confidentiality   20
  2. Compelling the appearance of an accused
    without arrest   21
Arrest   21
  1. Who has the power of arrest?   21
  2. What are the grounds for arrest?   22
  3. What are a youth's rights on arrest?   22
  4. What happens if the required procedures
    are not followed?   23
  5. The parents' rights when children are arrested   23
What rights do the police have on arrest?   24

Consulting with a lawyer on arrest or investigation	25
What happens next?	26

Chapter Three: Youth Court Proceedings — 27
Who are the parties?	27
Is there a right to an interpreter?	28
The duty of the witness to tell the truth	29
What are a youth's rights in obtaining a lawyer?	29
What happens on the first appearance in court?	31
Youths' rights on first and subsequent appearances	31
What happens if a youth is unsure as to how to proceed?	32
What happens when a youth is late for court or misses the court appearance?	32
Parents' rights when a child appears in youth court	33
Under what circumstances can a youth be tried in adult court?	34
What does it mean to be subpoenaed as a witness in youth court?	35

Chapter Four: Release Pending Trial in Youth Court — 36
What does the term "bail" mean?	36
What is the role of the police in determining release?	36
What happens at a bail hearing?	38
What does the *Young Offenders Act* say about bail?	39
Can a youth get psychological treatment or assessment at the bail stage?	40
What kinds of release orders are there?	41
What does it mean to "sign for" or "sign as a surety for" a youth?	42
What happens if the youth is charged with further offences while on bail for a previous offence?	43
What rights does a youth have at a bail hearing?	43
The role of parents at a bail hearing	45
What happens to youths who are not given bail by the youth court?	45
What happens next?	46

Chapter Five: What Happens When a Youth Pleads Not Guilty? — 48
Can what a youth tells a police officer be admitted into evidence at trial?	51

What happens if a youth has serious psychological problems? 52
In what circumstances is a charge withdrawn? 53
Can a finding of guilt be appealed? 53

Chapter Six: What Happens When a Youth Wishes to Plead Guilty? 55

Chapter Seven: What Happens When a Youth Is Sentenced? 57
Can a psychological assessment be obtained to assist in sentencing? 60
What sentences can be given to youths? 60
How long can dispositions last? 61
What dispositions are available in youth court? 62
  1. Absolute discharge 62
  2. Fines up to $1,000 62
  3. Compensation or restitution to injured parties 63
  4. Community service order 63
  5. Prohibition, seizure or forfeiture 63
  6. Detention for treatment 64
  7. Probation 64
  8. Custodial terms 65
  9. Other reasonable conditions 68
What happens if a youth wilfully fails to comply with a noncustodial disposition? 69

Chapter Eight: What Sentences Can Young Offenders Expect? 70
  1. Policy considerations 70
  2. General principles of sentencing in criminal matters 71
What rights does a youth have if unsatisfied with the disposition imposed? 73
  1. Sentence appeals 73
  2. The Review Procedure 74
    A. Reviews of custodial dispositions 74
      1. Youth court reviews 74
      2. Provincial director's recommendations 75
      3. Review boards 75
    B. Reviews of noncustodial dispositions 75

Chapter Nine: Some Other Matters 77
Does my child have a criminal record? 77
What happens if another person encourages a youth to
  disobey a court order, or to commit an offence? 78
Victims' rights in youth court 78

Chapter Ten: Sample Cases of Kids in Trouble 80
  1. A "Reverse Onus" Bail Hearing 80
  2. A Plea of Guilty Followed by a Crown Onus
     Bail Hearing 83
  3. A Plea of Guilty and a Noncustodial Disposition 86
  4. A Plea of Guilty and a Custodial Disposition 88
  5. A Plea of Guilty Followed by a
     Psychological Assessment 91
  6. A Transfer Application Granted 94
  7. A Trial in a Summary Matter 96
  8. A Trial in an Indictable Matter 99

Chapter Eleven: Last Words 105

Appendices
  (a) *Young Offenders Act* 107
  (b) Excerpts from the *Criminal Code* 167
  (c) Forms 191
  (d) List of Selected Summary, Hybrid and
       Indictable Offences 199

Endnotes 201

Foreword

It seems that everyone has an opinion about the *Young Offenders Act*, is prepared to debate its underlying principles and to comment on its present functioning. If a thorough reading and understanding of the legislation preceded discussion, it would be informed debate and fair comment.

Reading and understanding a statute, however, is often an arduous task, undertaken by a relatively small group of professionals who work with the legislation on a daily basis. If laws affect us all, there ought to be publications readily available that make statute law comprehensible to the general population.

Priscilla Platt has translated the formal statutory provisions of the *Young Offenders Act* into a language we can all understand. She has succeeded in presenting a thorough explanation of the themes and sections of the Act in a manner that is meaningful to professionals and lay persons alike. She has provided a helpful overview and a detailed examination of the Act for a broad range of professionals, parents, students, and other members of the public. Complex features of the legislation are made clear; formal legal terms are simplified.

Given the continuing curiosity about the content of the legislation and the private and public debate about its effectiveness, Priscilla Platt's contribution to our understanding of the *Young Offenders Act* is timely and valuable.

His Honour Judge Joseph C.M. James
Provincial Court (Family Division)
Toronto, Ontario

Acknowledgments

I am indebted to His Honour Judge J.C.M. James of the Ontario Provincial Court (Family Division) for his generous assistance and advice and for writing the Foreword, and to Roman N. Komar, Law Clerk to the Chief Judge of the Ontario Provincial Court (Family Division), who reviewed the text and made recommendations. I am also grateful to the Law Foundation of Ontario and the Ontario Arts Council for their financial support. Finally, I would like to express my appreciation to Mary Elizabeth Kneeland for editorial guidance, and to Mrs. Olive Young for her patience in typing this manuscript and its constant revisions.

Priscilla Platt
Priscilla Platt
March, 1987
Toronto

Introduction

The *Young Offenders Act* became law in 1984. It is a lengthy and complicated piece of legislation. Unfortunately, certain problems with the Act have been greatly publicized leaving the impression that it is unworkable and misguided. While it is not the purpose here to either criticize or praise the *Young Offenders Act*, it should be said that the Act is an effective tool in dealing with juvenile crime. From the public's point of view the Act can be used to punish offenders and deter them from further criminality. From a victim's point of view the Act protects victims' rights and gives them a voice in the proceedings. From the accused youth's point of view, the Act endeavours to ensure that not only are rights accorded, but that youths are fully apprised of those rights.

The purpose of this text is to review the provisions of the *Young Offenders Act* (See Appendix "A") in very general terms and in a practical context. Because this legislation deals with crime, I have endeavoured, where necessary, to explain some of the basic principles of criminal law. As well, in order to understand how this legislation has changed the way with which youths are dealt, reference is made to the previous legislation, the *Juvenile Delinquents Act*.

Youths and their families encountering the criminal justice system are often bewildered and afraid. With little experience in these matters, questions abound: What is the worst that can happen? How can we get help? How can we make our concerns known? Do we need a lawyer? If so, how do we get one? From time to time professionals, such as social workers and probation officers, required to administer various parts of the *Young Offenders Act*, are unfamiliar with the theory and practice of the criminal justice system and the formalities of the Act.

This text is set up to enable one to follow a young offender through all the steps from investigation and arrest to sentencing. While this is by no means a substitute for obtaining individual legal advice in a particular case, this book is intended to provide a general guide to what happens in youth court. In order to illustrate the principles and procedures outlined, sample fictional cases appear in Chapter Ten. It is hoped that after reading this material, many questions will have been answered and many fears allayed.

Clearly, a detailed review of all the law affecting young offenders is not contemplated here because the totality of the law is complicated and beyond the scope of this book. The law concerning young offenders is not only comprised of various pieces of legislation, but also of case law or precedents that interpret the legislation. Because the *Young Offenders Act* is a relatively new piece of legislation, not all its parts have been interpreted definitively by the courts. Moreover, the Act has recently been revised and amended. As a result, I have chosen to refer to the interpretation of the statute generally and not by a specific allusion to a particular case or precedent. The emphasis here is on a practical approach to the legislation and its implementation.

At the outset, it is important to emphasize that the *Young Offenders Act* is federal legislation that applies throughout Canada. It is basically *procedural* in nature, dealing with young persons involved in criminal activity. It reflects Parliament's intention to treat young offenders more like adults than was the case under the *Juvenile Delinquents Act*.

The *Criminal Code*, which is also federal legislation, and which therefore applies throughout Canada, creates offences and procedures for dealing with adults involved in criminal activity. Unless the *Young Offenders Act* states otherwise, the procedures of the *Criminal Code* apply. This is why, in the ensuing chapters, reference is continually made to both the *Criminal Code* and the *Young Offenders Act*. Moreover the offence with which a youth is charged does not generally originate in the *Young Offenders Act*, because it is primarily procedural, but in the *Criminal Code* or other federal legislation. For the purposes of this book, the most common offences originate in the *Criminal Code* or the *Narcotic Control Act*.

Offences created by provincial legislation such as truancy, careless driving, trespassing, and drinking under age are dealt with under provincial laws of procedure. Because of the number of different statutes involved throughout Canada, and because these offences tend to be of a less serious nature, I have chosen not to deal with these matters in this book. One should bear in mind, however, that there is a distinction between federal and provincial offences. While the *Young Offenders Act* applies throughout Canada, there are many regional differences. This is largely because the Act is administered provincially and each province, or indeed city, has different facilities and programs available to young offenders. As well, the interpretation of the various provisions of the Act and therefore the practice varies. What I have tried to do in this book is to indicate how the *Young Offenders Act* is implemented in most localities, so that individuals involved with this legislation can know generally what to expect. However, because my experience is based in Ontario, this text will in many instances reflect the Ontario practice.

Also, from time to time in these materials the pronoun "he" is used for convenience. It is intended that this be a reference to either a male or a female.

Chapter One

The *Young Offenders Act* and You

The basic differences between the *Young Offenders Act* and the *Juvenile Delinquents Act*

It is helpful to introduce the *Young Offenders Act* in the context of the former legislation, the *Juvenile Delinquents Act*. This provides a way of understanding the changes the *Young Offenders Act* has made, while at the same time highlighting the main areas in which the philosophy of the Act is expressed.

On April 2, 1984, the *Young Offenders Act* was proclaimed law throughout Canada. It replaces the seventy-five-year-old *Juvenile Delinquents Act*. It has in several areas ushered in a new era of responsibility for young persons involved in criminal activity.

1. To what offences and to whom does this Act apply?

The *Young Offenders Act* applies only to federal offences. In contrast to this, the *Juvenile Delinquents Act* applied to federal, provincial and municipal offences, and also to matters that were not crimes, such as sexual immorality. Offences were *delinquencies* and offenders were *delinquents,* or children "requiring help and guidance and proper supervision."

The *Young Offenders Act* has backed away from making young persons liable to punishment in circumstances in which adults would not be. For example, sexual immorality is not a crime, and therefore young persons cannot be charged with it. However, like adults, young persons can be charged with offences created in federal legislation such as the *Criminal Code* or the *Narcotic Control Act.* Provincial offences such as truancy and driving without a licence are punishable under provincial laws and not under the *Young Offenders Act.* Now youths are prosecuted only for *crimes,* in the same manner as adults. Because the Act applies only to federal laws, youths are not exposed to federal sanctions in matters that are not federal offences. Moreover, the terminology of the Act reflects an effort to treat young offenders as responsible persons. They are young *persons*, not children. They are *offenders*. It is indicated in section 3 of the Act, that young persons must bear responsibility for their conduct, and that society has the right to be protected from the offences of young persons.

Along with this new found accountability is the feeling that youths under twelve years of age should not be held responsible for criminal conduct. Therefore, while the *Juvenile Delinquents Act* applied in most provinces to those aged seven to fifteen, inclusive, the *Young Offenders Act* applied, initially to youths aged twelve to fifteen, and then as of April 1, 1985, to twelve to seventeen year olds inclusively throughout Canada. These age provisions refer to the date on which the alleged offence was committed.

2. Sentencing

By far the most important change of a practical nature is the judge's inability under the *Young Offenders Act* to sentence youths to indefinite custodial terms. Formerly, custodial terms generally were committals to industrial or training schools for indefinite or unspecified terms, lasting potentially until the juvenile's twenty-first birthday. In practice, this meant that the sentencing judge did not have to respond specifically to the crime, or *delinquency*, as it was called. Once an indefinite committal to an industrial or training school was made, the length of time depended on other factors and other officials. The *Young Offenders Act* gives sentencing back to the judiciary. Now a judge cannot sentence a youth to an unspecified custodial period, but must indicate the exact length of time.

Also, a judge must indicate the type of custodial facility in which the youth will be placed. The Act creates two levels of custody: open and secure. Open custodial facilities are generally unlocked facilities where youths can be given more freedom than in secure placements. In sentencing a youth to a period of custody a judge must indicate whether the sentence is to be served in an open or secure facility. Formerly, under the *Juvenile Delinquents Act* the sentencing judge did not have to specify in what kind of facility the youth was to be placed.

These changes reflect the intention of Parliament to deal with the sentencing of young offenders in a manner that more closely approximates the sentencing of adults.

3. Opening court and enlarging appeal rights

The shift of emphasis toward responsibility and accountability is reflected in other procedural changes under the *Young Offenders Act*. Formerly the public could be present in the courtroom when a child's case was being heard only if the judge allowed. Currently all youth court proceedings, like adult criminal proceedings, are open, so that the public is free to sit in on any proceedings in youth court, unless in very restricted circumstances the judge orders otherwise. A ban on publication of names or any information tending to identify the young person is in force.

The former Act restricted the rights of appeal while the current Act broadens these rights so that youths now have the same appeal rights as adults.

What is the philosophy of the Act?

The "declaration of principle" set out in section 3 of the Act, indicates the policy behind the legislation. Paragraph 3 (1)(a) states that while young offenders should "bear responsibility" for their offences, they should not be punished in "all instances" in the same fashion as adults. Paragraph 3 (1)(c) goes on to say that young offenders have "special needs and require guidance and assistance". Paragraphs 3 (1)(e) and (g) provide the young offender with all the rights that our law accords adult offenders. Moreover young persons have the right to be heard in any proceeding affecting them. Paragraph 3 (1)(f) indicates that youths have the "right to the least possible interference with freedom that is consistent with the protection of society, having regard to the needs of young persons and the interests of their families."

These paragraphs reflect Parliament's intention to treat young offenders similarly to adults in terms of rights, while — with respect to sentencing, recognizing their needs as youths.

Paragraph 3 (1)(b) indicates that society has the right to be protected from crime as well as the duty to take steps to prevent crime by young persons.

Paragraph 3 (1)(h) states that parents have responsibility for the care of their children and that young persons should only be removed from the care of the home where necessary. While acknowledging parental responsibility, the *Young Offenders Act* does not make parents responsible for the illegal conduct of their children. Responsibility for illegal conduct is placed squarely on the young offender. However, in recognition of the important role parents play in the development of young persons, the Act gives parents a special position in youth court proceedings. Parents are entitled under this Act to be notified of the release or detention of the youth by police, the date and place of the court hearing, to be present during youth court proceedings and to advise the court of their concerns.

It is clear from a review of section 3, that this Act seeks to balance the interest of young offenders and their families with those of society. This section is very important because the whole Act is required to be interpreted *liberally* in light of these provisions. Section 3 can potentially affect determinations regarding the youth at every stage of the process. However, the applicability of these provisions will depend on the facts of each particular case.

Are youth courts criminal courts or child protection courts?

Youth courts are not child protection courts, but sometimes the distinction is blurred and youth courts are asked to deal with the non-criminal problems of youths. Child protection matters are dealt with provincially in child protection or welfare courts (the name varies from province to province) through *civil*, as opposed to criminal, laws. If a child is misbehaving at home and the parent cannot or will not continue to provide care, a child protection agency can assume the parenting role. Sometimes a child protection court or welfare court decides these matters after a hearing. If part of the child's misbehavior includes the commission of criminal acts, the parent often brings to the youth court all the concerns the child protection agency, or court, would have heard. The parent wants the youth court to, in effect, force the child, through the *Young Offenders Act*, to do what could not be done under the civil child protection laws. This is because a breach of an order of the child protection court does not result in criminal sanctions, unless incidental to the breach, a crime is committed. However, when a youth breaches a youth court order very serious criminal sanctions can follow. In many instances, this is a grey area, but generally, youth court judges do not like to over-respond to what would otherwise be a minor criminal offence because the parent is having difficulty controlling the child.

Essentially, then, a youth court is a criminal court with the family playing a greater role than is the case in adult criminal court. Child protection agencies or child care facilities are in many instances, better equipped to deal with the emotional and familial problems of children than youth courts.

For example, when a child steals one dollar from a parent after an argument, he is technically committing a criminal offence. This may be the last act in a long line of other, albeit non-criminal, problems the parent has had with the child. The parent calls the police and the youth, who has never been charged with an offence before, is charged with the offence of theft. The parent may ultimately ask the youth court judge to place the child in a custodial facility for a "long time" to try to change the youth's general behavior, or to impose psychological treatment. The youth court judge, while considering the parent's concerns, will tend to want to treat the theft as an isolated and relatively minor offence. The court's reticence to look beyond the offence to the youth's other non-criminal behavior is particularly frustrating for the parent who has already made efforts through other routes which have been unsuccessful because of the child's lack of cooperation. Dealing with youths in these circumstances is both complex and difficult. This dilemma is raised very frequently in youth courts. A greater understanding of the criminal process and the provisions of the *Young Offenders*

Act may make the expectations of parents in these circumstances more realistic and thus reduce frustration. Therefore, while the needs of the youth and the interests of his family are factors that must be considered in youth court matters, these must be balanced with the rights of the accused youth and the basic function and purpose of a criminal court.

Chapter Two

The Role of the Police

Police officers are trained professionals whose job is to investigate crime and apprehend or arrest offenders. Many police departments have special squads, called youth bureaus, to deal with young offenders. The powers of police officers are indicated in the *Criminal Code* and extend to young offender matters.

Before a decision to lay a charge has been made

1. The duty to investigate
Police officers have a duty to investigate criminal activity. They investigate by attending at the scene or other place and obtaining physical evidence, such as fingerprints, and by speaking to persons who may have information concerning the crime. These persons may be witnesses, or they may be suspected perpetrators of the crime. It is in the interests of all of society that the public, which includes young persons, cooperate with police investigations by providing whatever information they can. However, when a young person is being investigated concerning a crime and that young person is a potential suspect, the law intervenes to provide certain rights.

A young person who is being investigated by the police as a suspect has to decide whether to talk to the officers about what happened. While young persons have a right to remain silent, they also have a right to speak freely to the police either to admit their guilt or to tell their side of the story (see page 22).

2. Police discretion
It is important to note that the police have some discretion as to whether a charge should be laid. This discretion is sometimes exercised alone or after consultation with the prosecutor. The *Young*

Offenders Act provides for, and many provinces have, programs designed to divert young persons who have committed crimes from youth court proceedings. These youths must admit their part in the crime and agree to submit to the alternative measures provided — such as community work. They never are charged and never attend youth court. These programs are largely designed for first offenders who have admitted their culpability in property crimes or in crimes of a less serious nature.

When a youth is offered diversion he ought to seriously consider whether or not he should take advantage of the procedure. The fact that a youth has participated in the diversion program can be considered on sentence for a future offence. This is so even after the youth becomes an adult. But if the youth is not guilty of the offence or has a good defence, no matter how technical, it is advisable to not choose diversion. In jurisdictions that do not have formal programs providing alternative measures, police still retain a discretion as to whether a charge must be laid. In restricted circumstances, some youth bureaus sanction giving youths warnings or cautions rather than laying a charge in every instance. When this is done, a private note is often kept of these warnings so that if subsequent incidents occur, charges will be laid.

The exercise of the police discretion not to lay a charge is dependent on a number of factors including:
- does the youth admit his crime
- is there remorse, are the parents or guardians concerned
- is the crime considered to be not very serious or of a technical nature
- does the youth have a prior record of offences, or prior warnings or cautions
- are others or adults jointly charged
- was the youth the main actor or just a follower
- is the family in control of the youth.

After a decision to lay a charge has been made

1. Confidentiality
The *Young Offenders Act* limits the release of information by police concerning investigations of young persons. Written information concerning investigations of youths is available only to spe-

cified interested parties and not to the public at large. For example, as of November 1, 1986, the amended provisions of the Act allow officers to disclose information to insurance companies investigating claims arising from offences committed by young persons. While newspapers can publish details of the *crime*, the *Young Offenders Act* in general prohibits publication of any information that would tend to identify the alleged *offender*. This has been argued by the police as a serious impediment in their efforts to apprehend alleged young offenders, particularly fugitives from detention or custodial facilities. Therefore, as of September 1, 1986, the Act was amended to allow for disclosure of identity by police and publication but only when permitted by a court order. Where the alleged young offender is dangerous to others or where publication of the identity will assist in apprehending the youth, these amendments allow the police to make application to a youth court judge for an order allowing publication of the identity.

2. Compelling the appearance of an accused without arrest
Where an officer has decided to lay a charge against a youth, there are instances when he nevertheless cannot arrest an accused. In these cases an appearance notice can be issued to the youth to compel his appearance in court. This may occur when the officer, with respect to certain offences of a less serious nature, does not believe that arrest is required to stop the repetition of the offence, preserve the evidence, establish the identity of the accused, or ensure the attendance of the accused in court.

Arrest
1. Who has the power of arrest?
Private citizens can make arrests in certain circumstances, for example, when they catch someone committing a crime. A citizen arresting someone in these circumstances is required to hold the person temporarily pending the arrival of the police. As well, citizens can lay charges on their own by attending at the office of the justice of the peace in the appropriate jurisdiction and swearing that facts exist to warrant a charge. The availability of these citizens' arrests and "private complaints," as they are called, extend equally to young offenders. The prosecution of private complaints is sometimes handled by the same prosecutor

who deals with police-laid charges. In some jurisdictions no prosecutor is provided for privately laid charges, so that the complainant must either do it himself or hire a lawyer. In all other respects the private-complaint trial and proceedings are identical to police-laid matters. It should be emphasized, however, that the overwhelming number of cases are proceeded with by the police.

2. What are the grounds for arrest?

A person is placed under arrest by being told by a police officer or arresting party that he is under arrest or by being physically restrained for the purpose of effecting the arrest. An individual can be arrested by a police officer who believes that a legal document called a warrant exists authorizing the arrest of that person. A police officer can also arrest a person whom he finds committing a criminal offence or in some cases where he has "reasonable and probable grounds" to believe that an offence has been committed. These provisions are set out in the *Criminal Code*, and apply to adults as well as to young persons. The definition of "reasonable and probable grounds" has been the subject of much judicial comment and generally it means a reasonably held belief or suspicion.

3. What are a youth's rights on arrest?

On arrest, a young person has the same rights as an adult accused under the *Canadian Charter of Rights and Freedoms* — that is to be told the reasons for the arrest and of his right to retain and instruct counsel without delay. In addition, the *Young Offenders Act* states that a youth on arrest must be told of the right to be *represented* by counsel and given an opportunity to do so.

If the police wish to ask the accused youth about the offence, he is usually advised, in the same manner as adult accused, of the right to remain silent and that anything said may be taken down in writing and introduced as evidence at trial. Youths also have the right to be told that a parent, or other "appropriate" adult or lawyer can be present to consult with prior to the taking of the statement and that any of these persons can be present during the taking of that statement. A youth who does not wish to take advantage of these rights will be asked to indicate this in writing prior to the taking of the statement. It cannot be emphasized too strongly that youths on arrest have every right to remain silent and to make no statement at all to the police. In addition, the fact that a youth has refused to make a statement cannot be used against the youth at trial and cannot be referred to in evidence. As indicated earlier, any information tending to identify the accused cannot, subject to certain exceptions, be published in the media. Also, while being held in the police station, the young person is generally entitled to be kept separate and apart from adult accused. If released by a police officer pending his court appearance, the youth has the right to have a parent notified of his release provisions and if detained, to have a parent advised of the place of detention and the reason for arrest.

4. What happens if the required procedures are not followed?
This is an extremely complex area of the law. For the purposes of this book, it may suffice to say that there may be repercussions. The *Canadian Charter of Rights and Freedoms*, for example, provides that where evidence is illegally obtained, that evidence *may* be excluded by a court. Therefore, evidence obtained as a result of an illegal arrest or unlawful search may be excluded. The *Young Offenders Act* also indicates that where statements are obtained without the requirements of the *Act* being followed, those statements will be ruled inadmissible by the court hearing the matter. However, failure to give notice to a parent as required under the *Young Offenders Act* usually does not affect the validity of subsequent proceedings.

It is important to note here that young persons should not react to perceived mistreatment by police with assaultive or abusive behavior. A youth who assaults an officer during an arrest or who obstructs an officer who is acting lawfully could be charged with further offences. The most prudent thing that a youth can do who believes he has been mistreated is to obtain advice from a lawyer.

5. The parents' rights when children are arrested
Generally, where a young offender is arrested and released by a police officer pending his court appearance, a parent is entitled to receive notice of the type of release given to the youth, which includes the date and place of the court appearance. If the young

offender is not released, but held in detention pending his court appearance, the parent has a right to notice of the arrest. The parent is also entitled to be present on arrest to consult with the child concerning the taking of a statement, if the child wishes this.

What rights do the police have on arrest?

Police officers have a right to know the name and address of the youth being arrested. They also have a general right to continue to investigate the young offender even after arrest. The officer may ask questions concerning the offence, and provided that all the proper procedures have been followed, may try to take a voluntary statement from the youth. He may search the youth if he believes that evidence may be found on his person, or may obtain a search warrant to search the premises where he believes evidence can be found.

Once the investigation is completed, police officers are empowered for certain offences to have the youth's photograph and fingerprints taken. That is to say, if the youth is charged with an offence that is indictable or with one that the Crown attorney (the prosecuting lawyer) can elect to proceed with by indictment, the police are authorized to take photographs and fingerprints for their records. All offences are characterized as either *summary*, or less serious; *indictable*, or more serious; or offences where the Crown attorney has the election whether to proceed summarily or by indictment. This last group of offences is often called *dual* or *hybrid*. To determine whether the offence is summary, indictable or dual, one must look to the original legislation, that is the *Criminal Code*, the *Narcotics Control Act,* or other federal statute. Most offences are either indictable or can be proceeded with by indictment. Where the youth is found not guilty of the offence, the fingerprints and photographs taken with respect to that charge are destroyed.

Fingerprints and photographs can be taken at the police station directly after the investigation or, if the youth is released, he can be required to sign a form indicating that he will attend at a certain place and time for the purpose of having these fingerprints and photographs taken. This form should be read carefully to ensure that the youth attends as required. Failure to attend is an offence in itself and the youth could be charged as a result of that omission.

For certain offences the arresting officer or the officer in charge must decide whether the youth should be released from the police station or be held in custody until he can be brought before a judge in order that a hearing can be held to determine whether release will be granted. For the very serious offences, police officers cannot release. The main factors to be considered when the power to release exists are whether the youth will attend court as required and whether it is in the public interest to release the youth. The public interest involves consideration of the nature of the offences and the likelihood that if released the youth will commit further offences. The most common forms of release by police officers are summonses, promises to appear and appearance notices. As a practical matter, if the parents are available and are prepared to take the youth home and the crime is not serious enough to require further measures most young offenders who have no record of previous offences are released from the police station. In these circumstances, the youth signs the form indicating that he agrees to attend court at a specific date and time. These forms may also contain a provision requiring the youth to attend a police station so that fingerprints and photographs can be taken. In some instances youths are held in custody for a bail hearing so that conditions of release can be imposed by the court because police officers are not empowered to do so. These conditions often assist the parents to gain control over their child and prevent further breaches of the law.

Consulting with a lawyer on arrest or investigation

Most youth bureaus have lists of lawyers who are prepared, day or night, to give initial advice, usually by telephone, to youths on arrest. This is a free service. If the youth does not know a lawyer, he can request the name and telephone number of one from the investigating officer. The youth is then given an opportunity to speak with the lawyer to obtain the information needed in order to know how best to proceed. The *Young Offenders Act* requires that all youths who wish a lawyer have one free of charge, regardless of their own or their parents' ability to pay. There are various procedures to follow in order to obtain a free lawyer (which will be dealt with in Chapter 3), but at the arrest stage these matters generally need not be addressed. The whole thrust of the *Young Offenders Act* is to see that youths have legal advice if they request it. It is important to reiterate here that provincial offences are governed by provincial legislation, which may or may not grant rights to counsel similar to the *Young Offenders Act*.

What happens next?

If the youth is released by the police, he will usually sign a form indicating his agreement to attend court at a specified date and time to set a date for trial or to plead guilty or to adjourn the matter. No witnesses will be in court on this occasion, nor can a trial be held on this first appearance. If the offence is one for which fingerprints and photographs are authorized, and they have not been taken prior to release, the youth will be required to attend at a police station on a specified date and time for that purpose. If the youth is detained in custody, he will be brought to court for his bail hearing.

Chapter Three

Youth Court Proceedings

Youth court proceedings are governed by the *Young Offenders Act*. It is important to reiterate, however, that according to section 51 of the Act, the provisions of the *Criminal Code* apply where there is no inconsistency or specific exclusion. This means that youth court proceedings are similar to adult proceedings unless it is otherwise indicated in the *Young Offenders Act*. Youth courts themselves are established by each province to hear young offender matters.

Who are the parties?
The judge presides over the proceedings and makes rulings concerning the facts and the law applicable in each case. The judge, whether female or male, is addressed as "Your Honour." (Often reference will be made to a decision of the "court" or an order of the "court"; in the context of youth court, the "court" means the judge sitting in youth court.)

Certain matters in youth court can be dealt with by justices of the peace. Justices of the peace are not judges. They can, however, fulfill a number of judicial functions under the *Young Offenders Act*. They *cannot* accept guilty pleas or hear trials. In many localities these persons preside over the setting of trial dates and at bail hearings. They also perform administrative functions. In youth court a justice of the peace is referred to as "Your Worship."

Cases in youth court are presented by the prosecutor. This individual is a lawyer, and is referred to as a Crown attorney or private prosecutor. Agents of the Attorney General who are not lawyers, called public prosecutors, can perform limited prosecutorial functions. In some localities these public prosecutors are in fact police officers.

The prosecutor represents the state or the "Crown," which is essentially the community interest. Under the Canadian criminal justice system, all accused are presumed innocent and the prosecutor must prove the guilt of the accused beyond a reasonable doubt.

The youth's interests are represented by a lawyer referred to as a defence counsel. The defence counsel's job is to act for the *youth*, not the youth's parents, and to advise the youth so that he is in a position to make informed choices.

Both defence counsel and Crown attorney are bound by professional responsibilities to both the court and their respective clients. The process in which cases are heard is adversarial. This means that both the defence and the Crown present their cases forcefully, and the judge ultimately decides the factual and legal issues.

The other persons in the court include court clerks who generally read the charges to the youth and fill out the documents; stenographers who make sure that all the words spoken are recorded, unless an independent recording device is in operation, so that transcripts of the proceedings can be made available; and court officers who assist the Crown attorney.

Courtrooms are forums where serious matters are heard. Therefore it is not acceptable to eat, drink, read newspapers or talk loudly or unnecessarily there. As a courtesy youths appearing in court should remember to dress appropriately.

Is there a right to an interpreter?

Youth courts provide access to court-appointed interpreters free of charge to ensure that an accused youth can understand the proceedings. Some courts even go so far as to provide interpreters for parents as well. Because of the unique position of the French language in Canada, many jurisdictions provide Francophone accused with the opportunity to have a trial in their own language. Full service in French is currently provided, for example, in Quebec, New Brunswick, Ontario and Manitoba. Any witness who testifies in youth court is entitled to do so in the language in which he is comfortable. An interpreter will be provided by the court to translate the testimony into the language in which the proceedings are being conducted.

The duty of the witness to tell the truth

Under the *Young Offenders Act*, all persons under the age of twelve who testify in youth court must be told about the duty to tell the truth and the consequences of not doing so. Where necessary, this must be explained to those under eighteen years of age as well. Witnesses promise to tell the truth based on an oath or, if they wish, on a "solemn affirmation." A witness taking an oath does so by swearing on the Bible to tell the truth. If the witness, based on conscientious scruples, does not wish to use the Bible, he can affirm. The wording of the affirmation is as follows:

> I solemnly affirm that the evidence to be given by me shall be the truth, the whole truth, and nothing but the truth.

The value of the evidence whether given under oath or affirmation is the same. It is a very serious offence not to give truthful testimony in court. Anyone who lies under oath or affirmation can be charged with perjury.

It should be noted that in dealing with very young children the judge must make special inquiries to ensure that they understand the nature of the oath or affirmation. If the judge decides the child does not understand this, the child may give unsworn or unaffirmed evidence. This type of evidence does not have the same value as evidence given under oath or affirmation.

What are a youth's rights in obtaining a lawyer?

The *Young Offenders Act* ensures that all youths, who so wish, are represented by counsel. It is important to note that the right to counsel applies only to federal offences; that is, for the purposes of this book, offences under the *Criminal Code* or under the *Narcotic Control Act*. Provincial offences, such as truancy, trespassing or careless driving, are governed by provincial legislation which may or may not provide for free legal counsel.

The *Young Offenders Act* indicates that every youth, regardless of the parents' or the young person's ability to pay, have a lawyer free of charge. However, the procedure to be followed for obtaining a free lawyer varies from province to province and sometimes within the province. Each province is responsible for making legal services available. Some provinces have legal aid plans whereby individuals can apply and, providing they meet the criteria — financial need, seriousness of the offence — obtain a piece of paper called a certificate, which they then take to any private lawyer who will accept it as payment. These programs generally require the cooperation of the parents in providing information. Lawyers who agree to act on a legal aid certificate must accept the fee as indicated in the legal aid tariff and no more.

Other provinces have a public defender system whereby lawyers who are hired full time provide the service for those in need. In provinces that have no legal aid or assistance programs, or where the youth has been refused aid through an existing program, the court must, if asked, order that youth be represented by counsel free of charge. The purpose of this provision in the *Young Offenders Act* is to ensure that youths do not go unrepresented.

The *Act* also provides that where there appears to be a conflict between the desires of the parents and those of the youth, the court may, on request, order that the youth have a free lawyer. Therefore, a youth will be represented by a staff lawyer, or a private lawyer, who agrees to accept the payment offered by the legal aid tariff, if a request is made to the court.

In circumstances where a lawyer is requested, and there is not time to provide one, for example, on arrest, or at a bail hearing, a duty lawyer is provided in most jurisdictions. These lawyers provide temporary advice and assistance to all youths who are unrepresented. They may advise the youth, usually by telephone, as to his rights on arrest. In court, they may advise the youth as to the rights and procedures available, and represent the youth at a bail hearing or for a guilty plea. These lawyers are available free of charge to any youth wishing to use the service.

A youth is not *required* to have a lawyer. Once the youth understands the right to counsel available under the *Young Offenders Act*, the provisions of the Act have been satisfied. It is fully acceptable, though perhaps not advisable, to appear before the court without counsel. It is also fully acceptable for youths or their parents to pay for a lawyer entirely on their own, and not use the free services offered.

If the youth is to be tried with other youths, that is, has

co-accuseds, each youth is entitled to be represented by *different* counsel. Because youths charged together frequently have opposing interests, it may be advisable that each youth obtain separate representation.

What happens on the first appearance in court?

Once the youth has been charged and released by the police, the forms served require the youth's attendance at a particular courthouse, on a particular date and time. It is generally necessary for the youth to attend *in person* at that time. If the youth cannot attend, a parent or other responsible person should come to the court and advise the judge of the circumstances of the non-attendance. If the youth does not attend or is late, serious consequences can follow.

Again, the first appearance in court is *not* a trial date and therefore there are no witnesses present or required at that time. Generally, a list of names of those accused required to appear in court is prepared. This does not necessarily reflect the order in which the names will be called. It is a good idea to advise the court attendant, or Crown attorney, that you are present and ready to proceed. You may then cut your waiting time considerably.

Youths' rights on the first and subsequent appearances

A youth attending court on a first appearance need not enter a plea of any kind. The judge on the first appearance is required to read the charge to the youth unless the youth waives (gives up) that right; and if he is not represented by a lawyer, to tell the youth of the right to be represented. If the youth chooses to plead guilty, he can do so with or without a lawyer, or with the assistance of the lawyer provided in youth court free of charge. If the youth is unrepresented, the judge must be satisfied that the youth understands the charge and that he can decide to plead guilty or not guilty. If the judge is satisfied, the charge is read to the youth; that is, he is "arraigned," and asked whether his plea is guilty or not guilty. If the youth pleads guilty, the Crown attorney then reads out a synopsis of the facts as alleged by the police. (See Chapter Six.) If these facts support the charge, the judge finds the youth guilty as charged. Thereafter an inquiry is made into the background of the youth to ascertain what sentence is appropriate.

What happens if the youth is unsure as to how to proceed?

This is very common. It is perfectly acceptable for the youth to ask that the matter be put over, or "adjourned" to another day to think about it, or to seek advice from private counsel or to apply for legal assistance. Alternatively, the youth may already know that he will be pleading not guilty. In that case, the court may set a trial date indicating that the youth will represent himself, or can adjourn the matter in order that the youth retain a lawyer. On a subsequent court date, when the youth has chosen a lawyer, the judge is advised by defence counsel, either in person or by letter, of dates when he is available for trial. The defence lawyer and the Crown attorney can usually agree upon a trial date on which all parties and witnesses are available. It is the judge who has the last say in fixing the date. It is evident from this, that it may take several appearances in court before a suitable trial date can be achieved. The length of time between the date when the youth is charged and the date of trial varies considerably with each locality. If a youth intends to obtain counsel, he can expedite the proceedings by taking the necessary steps as soon as possible, preferably before the first appearance date.

What happens when a youth is late for court or misses the court appearance?

It is important that the youth be on time for the scheduled appearances. If the youth is not present when his name is called in court, the judge may issue a court order for the arrest of the youth, called a "bench warrant." This warrant may or may not be rescinded, or withdrawn, if the youth appears after the required time. Therefore, if the youth knows that he will not make his appearance on time or at all, it is best to call the court ahead of time for directions on how to proceed. In addition to a warrant being issued by the judge for the arrest of the youth, a youth who fails to attend court can be charged with the new offence of "failure to appear in court." These matters are considered very serious by the courts. In cases where a court date is missed, it is always better to call the court or appropriate police division to ascertain how or when a youth can 'surrender' or turn himself in to the authorities because this is looked upon very favorably by the court. A youth who simply ignores a missed court appearance and waits to be arrested will likely find himself in detention (see Chapter Four.) Also, if the youth cannot attend because of school examinations or summer camp or illness, the courts are usually very understanding and will allow the parent or other adult to appear on behalf of the youth. In addition, if the offence is "summary," a responsible individual can attend youth court on behalf of the accused. However, all accused youths are required to attend youth court personally for their trial. Therefore, it is most important for youths, or persons attending youth court on their behalf, to observe the return dates and times strictly.

Parents' rights when a child appears in youth court

According to the Act, the parents or guardians have the right to be advised as soon as possible of the date when the youth is to be in court. Parents have the right to attend court each time with their child and advise or assist the youth and the court during that appearance. However, while parents are not required to attend court at any time with their child, the court may, if it feels it is in the interest of the youth, order the parent to attend at any stage in the proceedings.

That order must be served on the parent personally unless otherwise directed by the youth court. A parent who is ordered by the judge to attend court, and does not, is guilty of an offence and can be punished by the court. In those circumstances, the non-attendance can result in a warrant issued by the judge for the arrest of the parent. On arrest, the parent is brought before the court and once it is proved that the notice or the order was served, and no lawful excuse for non-attendance given, the judge in youth court can sentence the parent to a fine up to $2,000 or imprisonment for up to six months, or both.

While it is not required, many youth court judges prefer having at least one parent present on each appearance so that details can be ascertained readily when issues arise involving the background of the youth or the home situation. Also, when a parent is present, the judge can confirm that the family is aware of the full circumstances that brought the youth to court. Further, many youths are confused and inarticulate when in court, and parental guidance is of great assistance to them. Parents who cannot attend court with their child on each appearance ought to be present at the bail hearing and when the matter is ultimately tried, or when a plea of guilty is entered. It is, however, very difficult to know when a youth will decide to enter a plea of guilty. Because many judges prefer to have a parent present when a guilty plea is taken, if the parent is not present or cannot attend, the sentence hearing can be adjourned to give the parent an opportunity to be present.

Under what circumstances can a youth be tried in adult court?

When a youth is fourteen years of age or more and is charged with a very serious offence such as one where personal injury or death has resulted, the Crown attorney may determine that the matter ought to be tried in adult court. In these circumstances, an application must be made to the youth court under section 16 of the *Young Offenders Act*. A number of factors must be considered here, including the background of the youth, the seriousness of the alleged offence and the facilities available in both the adult and youth court system to deal with the young person if found guilty. When a transfer order is made, the youth is treated *in all respects* as an adult. Therefore the maximum sentence available is usually much longer than the maximum allowed under the *Young Offenders Act*. Moreover, the youth is tried according to the adult procedures, so that trial by judge and jury and preliminary, or pre-trial hearing are available. At a preliminary hearing a judge determines whether there is sufficient evidence to put the accused on trial. This procedure is not available to young offenders in youth court.

Transfer to "adult" court is not a Crown monopoly. Defence lawyers can ask for it as well. For example, a defence lawyer may advise his young client that a jury trial would be tactically advantageous and his client may then instruct the lawyer to seek a transfer order. It is, however, rare for a youth to seek transfer.

These applications are very often lengthy proceedings involving the filing of documentation and the testimony of several witnesses. Often a psychological examination of the youth is obtained in order to assist the court in determining whether transfer is appropriate. A pre-disposition report must be prepared and considered by the court. In view of the amount of personal information divulged at this sort of hearing the *Young Offenders Act* prohibits, on application by the young person, the publication in a newspaper or broadcast of *any* of the information heard. The transfer hearing is in general akin to a trial in the sense that each side can call witnesses and question them.

The judge must weigh all the evidence in light of the factors listed in section 16 and make a decision, indicating the reasons for the decision. Everything that is said during a transfer hearing is recorded. Either side may appeal the decision to the superior court of the province in which the transfer application was heard.

What does it mean to be subpoenaed as a witness in youth court?

When witnesses are required to give "material evidence" in court, a subpoena is issued and served on the person. This subpoena is a legal document ordering the person to attend court on a given date and time to give evidence. This may be on behalf of the defence or the prosecution.

Witnesses who are served with a subpoena should comply with it. If they do not, the party requiring their attendance can ask the court to issue an order, or warrant, for their arrest.

Often witnesses feel that attending court is inconvenient. This inconvenience in certain instances, may be lessened by contacting the party who issued the subpoena to see if arrangements can be made for attendance at a time when the witness will likely be required, as opposed to attending at the start of the court date and waiting until called.

Chapter Four

Release Pending Trial in Youth Court

What does the term "bail" mean?
For every charge that is laid, some provision must be made to compel appearance in court, or to release or detain the youth. It is important to be aware that once the youth is charged with an offence, and not detained, he is considered by the courts to be on "bail." While the term "bail" is no longer used in the legislation, it is a convenient word to use, understood by both professionals and laymen alike, to convey the concept of release pending trial. The significance of the fact that an accused is on bail once charged and released for an offence, is apparent when the relevant sections of the *Criminal Code* are reviewed.

Release provisions for youths are governed primarily by the *Criminal Code* because of the stipulation in the *Young Offenders Act* that the *Criminal Code* provisions apply unless otherwise inconsistent or excluded. Therefore when a youth is charged with a *federal* offence, that is, generally an offence under the *Criminal Code* or the *Narcotic Control Act*, the *Criminal Code* provisions govern release, whether it is release by a police officer or the courts.

Youth court judges generally hear young offender bail hearings, but justices of the peace can and do fulfill this function as well. Justices of the peace have fewer judicial powers than youth court judges. When a justice of the peace makes the decision whether or not a youth can be released from custody, the youth or prosecutor have the right to ask a youth court judge to decide this matter anew.

What is the role of the police in determining release?
As indicated in Chapter Two, police officers can, for many offences, though not the more serious ones, decide whether to release the youth or to hold the youth in detention for a bail hearing. The exercise of this discretion is governed by the *Criminal Code*. Police officers *cannot* release a youth on condition that he do or

not do certain things. Therefore, an officer who feels that something more than the basic form of release is required, may decide to hold the youth for a bail, or as it is commonly referred to, a show cause hearing. This is a youth court procedure wherein the judge or justice of the peace will decide whether the youth will be released and if so, the form of that release.

The officer may hold a youth in custody for a bail hearing because the youth's correct address or name cannot be ascertained, or because the youth has run away from a child protection agency placement or the parental home, or because the youth has a record of failing to appear in court in the past. These matters affect what is called the "primary ground" — whether the youth will attend court as required. When a youth has a prior record of offences, or is already on bail for another offence, the officer may feel that a bail hearing ought to be held because of the secondary ground, that is, there may be a reasonable belief that the youth would, if released, commit further offences, or because the release of the youth is otherwise not in the public's interest.

These two basic factors are the fundamental principles behind the bail legislation. Usually the officer will have consulted or tried to consult with the parents or guardians of the youth to assist in this decision.

If it is determined that the youth will be held for a bail hearing, the officer will prepare a summary for the Crown attorney including a synopsis of the allegations against the youth, the youth's background, the reasons for requesting the bail hearing and the type of release, if any suggested.

Often the police recommend some form of release with conditions. Sometimes a detention order is requested. The Crown attorney is not bound to accept the recommendations though this is often the case. The Crown attorney must review all the facts including the allegations on which the charge is based, together with the other information provided by the police, in order to decide whether to recommend to the court that some form of release be considered or to request detention. The judge or justice of the peace hearing the matter is not required to accept the recommendations of the police or the Crown attorney. The judge or justice of the peace will take all matters into consideration in arriving at an appropriate decision.

What happens at a bail hearing?

Very often defence counsel, on behalf of the youth, and the Crown attorney can agree to terms of release that the judge or justice of the peace is prepared to accept. If no agreement can be reached, or if the Crown attorney is seeking a detention order, a hearing will be held where the judge or justice of the peace will decide the matter. It should be noted here that an accused youth can agree to a detention order and, in these circumstances, a bail hearing will not be held and the youth will be detained. A youth may do this upon the advice of counsel because he does not believe he would be released. He may already be released on a number of bails or charged with escaping custody and would not be released because he is serving a sentence. As well, a youth may plead guilty at his first appearance in court for a bail hearing, and in these circumstances, if the matter of sentencing cannot be dealt with that day, the issue of bail will still have to be addressed. (See Chapter Six.)

Youth court bail hearings are governed by the provisions of the *Criminal Code*. Bail hearings are open to any member of the public who wishes to be present during the proceedings. Under the *Young Offenders Act*, publication of information tending to identify the accused is generally prohibited. Moreover, as a result of the provisions of the *Criminal Code* a youth at a bail hearing has the right on request to obtain an order from the judge or justice of the peace requiring a ban on publication of the evidence given during the hearing.

Except in certain circumstances, discussed at page 43, the Crown bears the burden of establishing the need for the desired form of release or detention based on the primary and secondary grounds, that is, the likelihood that the youth will attend court and whether it is in the public interest to grant release. At the beginning of the bail hearing, the Crown attorney either reads from the police summary or calls the officer involved in the case to give evidence. Either way the judge will hear the *allegations* that the police are making against the youth, the background of the youth, according to the police, and anything the police have learned about the youth that would reflect on the primary and secondary grounds.

The Crown attorney may have spoken to persons who have

opinions about the release of the youth, such as parents, guardians or social workers. These persons may testify, or may simply talk to the Crown attorney, who will then relay their concerns to the judge or justice of the peace. It is important to note that the bail hearing is *not* a trial and therefore witnesses may testify as to matters not within their *personal* knowledge. It is acceptable for the judge or justice of the peace to hear the person's belief as to what occurred or what others told him occurred. This sort of evidence is otherwise known as 'hearsay'. The whole procedure is designed to allow both sides to give enough information to the judge or justice of the peace so that a proper determination about release can be made. All of what is said during the hearing is recorded so that, on request, a transcript can be obtained. Any decision made by a youth court judge or justice of the peace concerning bail can be reviewed by, or appealed to, a higher court by the youth or the Crown attorney. A transcript of the original proceeding is required in order for the review to take place. It is unclear whether the *Young Offenders Act* provides the right to be represented by a lawyer free of charge, on a bail review.

What does the *Young Offenders Act* say about bail?

It may be said that the *Young Offenders Act* by virtue of some of its policy statements leans toward the release of youths. I am referring here to paragraphs 3(1)(f) and (h), which state that:

> ... the rights and freedoms of young persons include a right to the least possible interference with freedom that is consistent with the protection of society, having regard to the needs of young persons

and that:

> parents have responsibility for the care and supervision of their children, and for that reason, young persons should be removed from parental supervision either partly or entirely only when measures that provide for continuing supervision are inappropriate.

This does not mean that where parents are no longer willing to care for their child that the youth will be detained in custody. Very often child protection agencies will take the youth into care if release by the youth court is otherwise appropriate. These paragraphs go on to provide that the law regarding young persons must be liberally construed in accordance with these principles.

Recent amendments provide that in lieu of detaining a youth, where a responsible person is willing to care for the youth pending trial, and the youth is agreeable, a judge can release the youth to that person's care when the youth signs an undertaking, or promise to the court. This type of release is to be granted only where detention would otherwise be appropriate. Further amendments to this section require the youth *and the responsible adult* to agree in writing to abide by certain conditions as imposed by the court before release is granted. They also create a procedure for terminating the undertakings. As well, a new offence of failing to comply or abide by the conditions of release has been created. Therefore, not only the youth, but the *adult* who undertakes to care for the youth, could be found guilty of this offence.

The applicability of these provisions of the *Young Offenders Act* will vary with the facts and circumstances of each case. With these exceptions, the *Young Offenders Act* does not refer to release, so that the adult provisions contained in the *Criminal Code* apply. It is important to note that, while the adult legislation applies, youths held in detention awaiting a hearing are generally held separate and apart from adults.

Can a youth get psychological treatment or assessment at the bail stage?

While the Act deals with the circumstances when medical and psychological assessments can be obtained, it does not specifically allow the court to order these assessments to assist the judge or justice of the peace in deciding whether to release a youth on bail. Therefore it is doubtful (subject to future judicial rulings) that the court has the power to require that a psychological assessment be done at the bail hearing. However, if other issues, such as fitness to stand trial exist (see Chapter Five), a psychological assessment may be ordered at this stage. Nevertheless, these reports can be ordered at many other stages of the process, notably after a guilty plea (see page 60). There is, of course, nothing to prevent an accused or his family from seeking psychological assistance outside of the court system and without a court order. This can be done at any time.

What kinds of release orders are there?

The judge or justice of the peace at a bail hearing can order a youth released on an undertaking (or promise) to appear in court, with or without conditions, or on a recognizance, with or without a surety, which is a promise based on an amount of money, with or without deposit of funds and with or without conditions. The judge or justice of the peace can also order a youth detained in custody pending trial. If the parent or guardian feels that court-ordered conditions will assist him/her in maintaining control over the youth, the judge or justice of the peace will usually consider this. For example, the court could order the youth to stay away from certain individuals or certain locations, to obey a specified curfew, to reside at a particular place and to obey certain house rules, to report to a police station or to attend school or counselling.

The judge or justice of the peace can, of course, impose these conditions on his own inclination and without a request from the family. If conditions are imposed, the youth must abide by those rules. A copy of the release order with conditions is given to the youth and if he breaches any of the terms while on release, a further charge called "fail to comply" can be laid.

The imposition of conditions is designed to ensure attendance in court or to prevent further breaches of the law. The conditions are generally in force until the trial, including sentencing, is completed. It should be noted that it is possible to change these conditions or any bail order, in youth court (without the necessity of a bail review) at any time if the Crown attorney consents to the change and the judge or justice of the peace agrees. Also the judge hearing the trial has the power to revoke a release order and place a youth in detention, to release a youth from detention, and to change the conditions of release. This procedure is unusual and requires that there be good grounds for the change.

If the youth is ordered to sign his *own* recognizance in a specific amount of money, usually without deposit, and the youth after release does not appear in court as required, that amount of money is at risk and may become owing to the province.

What does it mean to "sign for" or "sign as a surety for" a youth?

This means that the youth is being released on a form of release called a recognizance and that the person who signs the recognizance is agreeing to act as "surety" in order for the youth to be released from custody. In these circumstances the youth court judge or justice of the peace having heard the facts, has decided that the youth can only be released if someone, probably a parent, is prepared to sign a piece of paper known as a recognizance, in front of a justice of the peace, indicating that the signer may forfeit a fixed sum of money if the youth fails to attend court as required. If the judge or justice of the peace has indicated that the money need not be deposited, then no money changes hands at this time. The judge or justice of the peace may go on to say that a particular person is "approved" by the court, so that that individual need not be required to prove financial worth. If the court has *not* ordered that a particular person is "approved," financial worth can be proved to a justice of the peace by showing a current bank book, with the funds in it, or proving property ownership or worth in other ways. If a deposit of money is required, a certified cheque or money order must generally be given to the justice of the peace in order to effect the release of the youth.

If the youth fails to attend court as required, the Crown attorney may ask for an "estreatment" of the bail. This means that the amount indicated in the recognizance is put at risk. Ultimately, a separate hearing is held to determine whether the person who signed the recognizance must either pay or forfeit the face amount to the province. If the youth appears in court as required, the surety is entitled to be relieved of the recognizance when the whole matter including sentencing is completed.

In youth court, judges or justices of the peace generally impose this form of release in addition to conditions to give the surety, usually the parent, more control over the youth than conditions without a surety would. It allows control because if any of the conditions are broken, or if the surety is having difficulty with the youth, and no longer wishes to be a surety, that person can attend at the particular courthouse where the matter arose and advise the justice of the peace or judge that he no longer wishes to be a surety. Once this is done, there is a warrant out for the arrest of the youth, who is now in the position of not having the bail order satisfied. The youth, on arrest, will remain in custody for a new bail hearing. It may be that, given the circumstances of the actions taken by the surety, bail will be denied at the new hearing and the youth will remain in detention. Moreover, if a youth breaches a condition of release, a new offence has been committed. It can readily be seen, then, that a surety release with conditions is desirable from a parent's or guardian's point of view.

What happens if the youth is charged with further offences while on bail for a previous offence?

As has been indicated, it is an offence to breach a condition of release ordered by the court. If the youth breaches the conditions of his former release and is charged with that new offence or any other new offence while on bail, the police officer will likely hold the youth for a bail hearing. Moreover, if the youth is held for a bail hearing in circumstances where it is alleged that a new offence was committed while on bail (that is, *any* form of release) for an earlier offence, the youth will have much more difficulty obtaining a release. The youth will generally be in what is called a "reverse onus" situation which means that the *youth*, not the Crown attorney, will now bear the burden of proving that on the primary ground, attendance in court, and on the secondary ground, the public interest, detention is not necessary. In other words, it will be assumed that the youth should be detained, unless he shows why he should not be.

In many cases, a youth in these circumstances is detained. Therefore accused youths should be aware that once they have been released on a charge and are awaiting trial, they ought to be on their best behavior or their liberty is at risk.

What rights does a youth have at a bail hearing?

In general, a youth held in custody by the police has the right to be brought before a judge or justice of the peace within twenty-four hours, or as soon as possible thereafter, to be dealt with. The accused youth or the prosecutor can apply to the youth court for an adjournment of the bail hearing for up to three days without the consent of the other party. If this application is granted, the youth would remain in custody pending the adjournment.

The youth at a bail hearing has the right to be represented by counsel, to be advised of that right, and to be given a reasonable opportunity to obtain counsel. In jurisdictions where a public defender system is in use, a staff lawyer is provided to the youth to act at the bail hearing. In jurisdictions where legal assistance programs exist, many youths, because of the short notice involved, do not have counsel of their choice available at the bail hearing. In these circumstances, the youth can usually use the services of the duty counsel, who is a lawyer provided free of charge for that purpose. A youth who wishes to wait for a particular counsel to attend, can adjourn the matter to another day when that counsel can attend.

If the youth wishes to wait for counsel of his choice, he would be required to remain in custody until the date set for the bail hearing. Alternatively, the youth can proceed without counsel, although this is not usually advisable. Regardless of how representation is provided at the bail stage, many youths are released from custody without requiring a full hearing by simply agreeing to conditions of release negotiated between the defence counsel and the Crown attorney and accepted by the court.

The parents, as has been indicated, are not required to be present in youth court, but a youth may request that a parent be present for his bail hearing and the judge may then order the parent to attend. It may be that the judge will not be willing to hold a youth in custody until the parent can attend pursuant to the court order, unless of course the youth is agreeable to that.

The youth can, alone or through counsel, cross-examine or question the Crown's witnesses or call his own witnesses. The youth also has the right to remain silent at the hearing or to testify on his own behalf. A youth who testifies cannot be asked about the offence with which he is charged. After all the evidence has been heard, submissions are made by the Crown attorney and the defence counsel. The judge then makes his decision. If the decision is one with which the youth disagrees, the right of appeal or review can be utilized.

The role of parents at a bail hearing
As has been indicated earlier, a parent must be notified of the arrest and place of detention of the youth and of the date and place of the court hearing. The parent can attend the court proceeding and testify as a witness if the defence or Crown wishes, or provide input to the proceedings as requested or desired.

What happens to youths who are not given bail by the youth court?
Youths who are not granted bail, and who have exhausted their review rights, usually remain in detention until the trial is completed, and if found guilty, sentenced. Detention for youths is generally in a facility separate and apart from adults. Most of these facilities provide some form of recreation, schooling and guidance or supervision, with the specific programs offered varying from jurisdiction to jurisdiction. Many allow scheduled visits from family and friends. Some jurisdictions provide different settings for youths in detention. In Ontario, for example, youths in detention may be placed in unlocked group homes in community settings or in more secure locked facilities. Moreover, youths in detention may be allowed out in the community in group outings or individually for a particular purpose. However, the opportunities for leaving the place of detention vary with the locality. The time spent in pre-trial detention is taken into consideration by most judges on sentence if the youth is ultimately found guilty.

The length of pre-trial detention will vary with the type of offence and the locality in which the matter is tried. Most courts make every effort to accommodate persons in custody by giving them priority in the setting of early trial dates. Of course, if the youth, once detained, decides to enter a plea of guilty, rather than require a trial, this can usually be arranged at any time.

It is important to note that once a youth is detained in custody, regardless of the place of detention, he cannot leave that facility without permission, nor can the youth who is given permission to leave temporarily stay away longer than allowed. These actions can result in the laying of a further charge of escaping lawful custody.

What happens next?

Once the bail issue has been determined, a trial date will be set either at that time or on a subsequent day. The reasons for the adjournments vary, but often it is to obtain counsel. When the youth obtains counsel and a trial is requested, a date convenient to all parties, including the witnesses who will be required, is set. That trial date is fixed and can be changed only upon application to the youth court by the defence counsel or the Crown attorney. The defence counsel or Crown attorney must bring the application well before the trial date and show good grounds for seeking the change, or the request will be refused. After the trial date is set, the witnesses, are supoenaed and the case is prepared for trial.

Prior to the trial, a youth, and perhaps the parent or guardian, will want to discuss the case with the defence lawyer. Often the lawyer has already met with the Crown attorney who has disclosed the details of the evidence the Crown proposes to call against the youth. The defence lawyer and Crown attorney may have discussed the possibility of a guilty plea, the charges to which the youth may plead guilty, and what sentence the Crown will be seeking. It may be that the youth, after discussing the matter realistically with the defence lawyer, will decide to plead guilty.

It is important to note, again, that the defence lawyer acts for the *youth*, and not for the parents. Moreover, while the youth is guided by the lawyer, in the final analysis, the youth is the one who generally makes the decision whether to plead guilty or not guilty.

The Crown bears the burden of proving the accused's guilt beyond a reasonable doubt. Even if a defence lawyer believes a youth to be guilty, he may quite properly advise the youth to plead not guilty if he believes that this course of action is in the interests of the youth. This forces the Crown to prove the case against the youth beyond a reasonable doubt. The plea of "not guilty" does not mean the same thing as "innocent." Indeed, there is no such plea as "innocent" in criminal law. Therefore, a plea of "not guilty" is *not* a public assertion of innocence. "Not guilty" merely means that the accused or the defence lawyer believes that the prosecution cannot prove its case beyond a reasonable doubt. Thus, the lawyer can ethically advise his or her client to plead "not guilty" and a young person can, with a clear conscience, stand up and say "not guilty."

Chapter Five

What Happens When A Youth Pleads Not Guilty?

Youth court trials are the same as trials held in adult court in the sense that the rules of evidence and procedure are the same, unless the *Young Offenders Act* states otherwise. An important difference is that for certain offences an adult would have the right to a pre-trial or "preliminary" hearing and the right to a trial by judge and jury. A youth has no such rights. Therefore trials for youths are heard by a youth court judge in one hearing (although this is always subject to future judicial rulings). It sometimes happens that, because of scheduling difficulties, matters set for trial are not reached or are reached but not completed. If this happens, the trial is adjourned to another day.

The *Young Offenders Act* restricts the ability to publish any information that will tend to identify the youth charged *or* any young persons or children (those under twelve years of age) appearing as *witnesses*. It is an offence to do so. As a result of this, newspapers can publish accounts of youth court trials, but must, unless otherwise ordered, refrain from using the names, addresses or other descriptions that would identify the young persons or children involved.

A youth court trial can be closed to the public if, in restricted circumstances, the presence of the public would be harmful to a child or young person, either as accused or witness. Whether the trial is conducted in an open or closed court, all words spoken are recorded.

Before the trial begins the judge may make inquiries as to who is present with the youth, such as parent or guardian, and the age of the youth, to ensure that the accused youth is over twelve and under eighteen years of age. If the parent is not present, the judge might inquire whether the parent has been notified in accordance with the *Young Offenders Act*. If proper notice has not been given, the judge may adjourn the matter so that notice can be given. Trials can proceed without the presence of the parent and generally, lack of notice will not lead to a dismissal of the charges. If the youth is not represented by counsel, the judge may make sure that the youth understands the right to have a free lawyer. If it is apparent that the youth would have had counsel if he had understood these rights, the trial will very likely be adjourned so that the youth can obtain counsel.

A youth court trial begins by the judge or clerk reading the charges to the youth; that is, "arraigning" the accused. With respect to certain charges, the Crown attorney will then be asked: "How do you elect to proceed?" This is done because the charge that the youth faces, as indicated in the federal statute, that is, the *Criminal Code* or *Narcotic Control Act,* is a summary conviction offence, an indictable offence, or an offence punishable summarily or by indictment, that is, a dual procedure offence. Generally, summary offences are considered less serious and indictable the most serious. Many offences fall in between, so that the Crown attorney is given the choice how to proceed. If the Crown attorney does *not* make a choice or an "election," then the offence is considered to be a summary matter.

In youth court, the indictable procedure is no different than the summary mode, but it provides greater flexibility on sentencing. If the Crown attorney elects to proceed by indictment, then the maximum sentence available is longer than that available by the summary procedure. As well, a finding of guilt on an indictable offence results in a longer required period of "good behaviour" before the records must be destroyed (see Chapter Nine). Therefore, if the facts alleged appear to be more serious than is usual, or if the youth has a lengthy prior record of offences or pending charges, the Crown attorney may feel it is prudent to proceed by indictment, so that in the event of a finding of guilty, a longer or more severe sentence can be requested.

Once the Crown attorney makes the election, the judge will usually inquire whether the youth understands the charge that was read. The judge or clerk then asks the youth whether the plea is guilty or not guilty. If the youth indicates "not guilty," either the Crown attorney or the defence counsel can at this juncture request that the judge order that all witnesses who will be testifying remain outside of the courtroom, so they do not hear each other's testimony. It should be noted that an accused young person has the right to remain in the court throughout the entire proceedings.

The Crown attorney starts by calling the Crown witnesses. The Crown attorney asks questions of the witnesses making sure he does not suggest the answer by the question. This is important because it is a rule of procedure that one cannot "lead" one's own witness. The questioning of one's own witness is called "examination-in-chief." Once the Crown attorney has concluded the examination-in-chief of a witness, the youth, or defence counsel on the youth's behalf, has an opportunity to question the witness. This is called "cross-examination" and can be done much more freely. For instance, during this type of questioning, it is entirely proper to suggest answers to the witness. The purpose of cross-examination is not only to attack the evidence given against the youth, but to bring out evidence favorable to the youth that has not been elicited by the Crown attorney.

When the Crown attorney has called all his witnesses and they have been examined and cross-examined, and in some cases re-examined, the court will be advised that the case for the Crown is completed. At this time the defence might seek a dismissal of the charges, because even if the Crown's evidence is believed, it is still too weak to prove the youth is guilty beyond a reasonable doubt. Far more frequently the defence will elect either to call no witnesses or to call its witnesses. It is a cornerstone of the criminal justice system that an accused can choose not to testify or not to call any witnesses and to make the Crown attorney prove the charge beyond a reasonable doubt.

While a youth has the right to not testify at his trial, the decision *to* testify is also a right. The defence is free to call witnesses, whether or not the accused youth decides to testify. Any defence witnesses called are examined in chief by defence counsel, or by the youth if unrepresented, in the same manner as the Crown attorney examined his witnesses, that is, without using leading questions. The Crown attorney then has the opportunity of cross-examining the defence witnesses including the accused youth, if called. It is a basic principle that the Crown (or even the judge) can never call the accused youth to testify against himself. It should be noted here that the judge is entitled to, and often does, ask questions of witnesses during a trial, usually to clarify testimony. The judge also makes rulings as to whether certain evidence is admissible. After the defence has called all of its witnesses, the judge may in restricted circumstances, allow the Crown to call witnesses in reply.

When all the evidence has been heard, the judge will ask for "submissions" from both sides. Submissions are statements made by the defence counsel and the Crown attorney to the judge about their respective views of the evidence given and of the applicable law. Youths have available to them all the defences that are available to an accused of any age under the criminal law. It is the role of the judge to decide what facts he finds to have been proved and to make rulings on the law. For instance, the judge makes findings as to the credibility of individual witnesses. He may accept all, none, or part of the evidence of a particular witness. The judge then applies the law as he interprets it to the facts as he has found them and determines whether the youth is guilty or not guilty. A finding of "guilty" means that the youth is found guilty beyond a reasonable doubt. A finding of "not guilty" means that the Crown attorney has not proved the youth guilty beyond a reasonable doubt. It is not the same as a finding that the youth is innocent.

If the youth is found guilty the judge has the power, where the youth has been released on bail on the charge, to revoke bail and place the youth in custody. Though this is rarely done, some charges warrant this procedure. As well, the trial judge has the power to release a youth from detention prior to sentencing.

Can what a youth tells a police officer be admitted into evidence at trial?

This matter requires special mention because the *Young Offenders Act* indicates that statements given by youths on arrest can be adduced at the trial only in certain circumstances. This is a very complex area.

A statement given to a police officer may include anything revealed by the accused, whether it was just an oral statement or a written one, and whether signed or unsigned. Contrary to what many people think, an unsigned statement can still be admissible in court. In general, statements given by any accused person on arrest are admissible in court once the Crown attorney proves beyond a reasonable doubt that they were given freely and voluntarily. With respect to young offenders, however, before a statement can be given in evidence at trial, the Crown attorney must prove also that the youth was told and understood, before he gave a statement, that he had a right to consult with a lawyer, parent or other "appropriate" adult person. Moreover, the youth must have been given an opportunity to make the statement in the presence of that adult, parent or counsel. If the youth wishing to make a statement consulted with the "appropriate" adult and made the statement in front of the adult, the statement will likely be admitted into evidence at trial. However, if the youth wishing to make a statement either will not or cannot consult with the "appropriate" adult, the police officer will ask the youth to sign a paper indicating that he has been advised of his rights and agrees to give them up. The youth may do away with both rights only in writing. If the youth does not "sign away" his rights any statement made cannot be used against him in court. The Crown attorney usually proves that the statement is voluntary and in compliance with the *Young Offenders Act* by calling as witnesses all the police officers or persons in authority who had dealings with the youth. If the *Act* is not complied with, or the statement is not proved voluntary, it will not be admitted into evidence at the trial. A youth, or defence counsel on his behalf, can, however, agree that the statement made was voluntary and in compliance with the *Act* and therefore not require the Crown attorney to prove this.

What happens if a youth has serious psychological problems?

In order to proceed to trial, a youth must be "fit" or able to stand trial. The legal test for fitness is based on a determination that the youth understands the charge and the reason for the proceedings and can give instructions to his lawyer. If there is doubt about the youth's fitness, a psychological report can be ordered. If the report indicates that the youth is not fit to stand trial, a hearing will be held so that a youth court judge can decide that issue. If the youth is found by the judge to be unfit, the youth will be detained in a treatment facility for an indefinite period until the time when the youth becomes sufficiently mentally fit to stand trial.

Youths who are fit, but who allege that at the time of the offence they were insane — that is, "incapable of appreciating the nature and quality of an act or omission or of knowing that an act or omission is wrong" owing to a disease of the mind — within the meaning of the *Criminal Code*, can use the defence of insanity. If this defence is successfully used, the youth is found "not guilty by reason of insanity." Youths in this situation are not automatically free to leave the courtroom. The result of this finding is that the youth is held in a psychiatric facility for an indefinite period until a review board decides that treatment is no longer necessary.

In what circumstance is a charge withdrawn?

The Crown attorney has the discretion to proceed with the charge or to ask the court to withdraw it. Once asked to do so the court must withdraw the charge. This means that the youth does not have to face the charge at all and all records concerning the charge are ultimately destroyed. This can be done in circumstances where the Crown attorney, before the taking of a plea, feels that the charge, for various reasons, cannot be proved. It can also happen that charges are withdrawn on humanitarian grounds, when the charges are very minor and the repercussions of a trial or a finding of guilt would work a disproportionate hardship.

Another situation where there would be a withdrawal is illustrated in the following example. Where there has been a theft from a retail store and the goods are found in the possession of the accused, charges of theft and possession of stolen goods are laid. If the youth pleads guilty to one of the charges, the Crown attorney will withdraw the other charge because a person cannot be found guilty of two different charges arising from the same incident.

Can a finding of guilt be appealed?

Youth court decisions can be appealed and youths have the same appeal rights as adults. A youth can appeal both a finding of guilt and sentence. An appeal must generally be launched within a fixed period of time from the date the sentence is imposed.

Appeals are based, for the most part, on a transcript of the evidence given and judgment made at the trial. A youth who is sentenced to a custodial term after a finding of guilt, can apply for bail while awaiting the appeal. The *Young Offenders Act* does not give a youth the right to counsel free of charge on an appeal so that each province will determine how legal services are given to youths in these circumstances. Appeals are very technical and beyond the scope of this book. One should always seek the advice of legal counsel when considering an appeal.

Chapter Six

What Happens When A Youth Wishes To Plead Guilty?

An accused youth, as has been indicated, can choose to plead guilty at any stage of the proceedings and on any appearance in court. For example, if a youth is held in custody for a bail hearing, he can plead guilty at that time, instead of having a bail hearing. As well, a youth can plead guilty on a trial date.

If the youth is unrepresented by a lawyer, or seems to be rushing into the guilty plea, the judge may make more than the usual inquiries. If it appears that the youth wishes to plead guilty "to get it over with" or to avoid coming to court on other occasions or because someone told him he must, the plea of guilty will *not* be accepted. Moreover, a plea of guilty "with an explanation" is also *not* acceptable in youth court.

When a youth wishes to plead guilty on a first appearance in court, the judge is required to read the charge to him and if he is not represented by a lawyer, advise him of his right to have a lawyer represent him. On any court date if the youth is unrepresented by a lawyer, the judge must, before accepting a plea of guilty, ensure that the youth understands the charge, and explain the right to plead guilty *or* not guilty. If the judge feels the youth does not understand the charge he is facing, the youth will not be allowed to plead guilty and the matter will proceed to trial.

If the youth understands the charge, and the judge is satisfied that a plea of guilty should be taken, the judge will usually ascertain whether a parent or other appropriate adult is present. If no one is with the young person, the judge may decide to put the matter over to a date when the parent can be present. On the other hand if the judge feels that in all the circumstances the presence of the parent is not required, the youth will be allowed to enter the plea of guilty at that time.

Once it is determined that the plea of guilty is appropriate, the charge will be read to the accused youth, that is, the youth will be "arraigned." The Crown attorney will then be asked, in the case of certain offences (dual offences), "How does the Crown elect to proceed?" The Crown attorney will either say "summarily" or "by indictment." (See explanation for this in Chapter Five.)

The youth will then be asked how he pleads, guilty or not guilty. If the plea is guilty, the Crown attorney will read out a brief summary of the facts as alleged by the police. The youth must listen carefully to those facts because the judge will ask him if those facts are correct. The youth or defence counsel on behalf of the youth will then, if those facts are correct, say "substantially correct." This means basically correct. No youth should ever accept facts that are not true.

The court must be advised of any matters that cannot be admitted. If those matters are not material, that is, do not go to guilt or innocence, then the plea will likely be accepted. When this is done the judge must find the young person guilty of the offences. If, however, those matters are material, then the judge must 'strike' the plea of guilty and the youth will be required to proceed to trial. It should be noted that under the *Young Offenders Act*, the term "convicted" is not used. Unlike adults, young persons are "found guilty," not convicted.

If the guilty plea is accepted and the youth is found guilty, the sentencing hearing will begin. If sentencing cannot be dealt with on that day, and the youth has not had a bail hearing, the release of the youth will be determined at this time. If the youth pleaded guilty to the charge after being released, the judge hearing the matter has the power, though infrequently used, to revoke the bail and place the youth in custody pending sentence. This may be done because of the seriousness of the charge seen in light of the youth's prior record of offences. If the youth was detained in custody prior to the time when the plea of guilty was made, and sentence is delayed, the judge also has the power to release the youth from custody pending sentence.

Chapter Seven

What Happens When a Youth Is Sentenced?

While the sentencing process can take place in open court, recent amendments to the *Young Offenders Act* allow the youth court judge to exclude the public from a sentencing hearing. The sentences available to young persons are called "dispositions" under the *Act*.

It should be noted here that while the Crown attorney very often seeks a certain disposition, the judge may or may not agree. The judge will impose a disposition that is fit considering all the circumstances. Indeed, even where the Crown attorney and defence counsel jointly ask the judge to impose a particular disposition, the judge will not necessarily do so. The judge must consider all the factors and arrive at an appropriate disposition.

When a youth is found guilty, whether after a plea of not guilty or a plea of guilty, the judge will usually ask the Crown attorney whether there is a prior "record." This inquiry refers to whether the youth has been found guilty before. Prior charges that did *not* result in findings of guilt are *not* part of the record. Moreover, if the youth is awaiting trial on other charges, whether or not they arose before or after the charge for which the youth is being sentenced, these charges cannot be considered on sentencing. It would appear, however, that the fact that a youth has previously been part of an alternative-measures or diversion program can be indicated at a sentencing hearing for a subsequent offence.

If there has been a prior finding of guilt, regardless of sentence, then the police, using the name and birth date of the youth, are usually able to ascertain the details after the youth has been arrested, and provide them to the Crown attorney. This is very often in the form of a computer printout. This record must be shown to the youth or his defence counsel to ensure that it is correct and admitted *before* the judge is advised of it. If the youth disputes the details of the record, the Crown attorney can accept what the youth indicates, or seek an adjournment to prove the record according to the procedure in the *Criminal Code*. If the record is admitted, it is shown to the judge who then asks both the defence counsel and the Crown attorney for "submissions" or suggestions to the court as to what sentence is appropriate.

Sentencing young offenders is perhaps the most difficult and most important duty facing a judge. It is also the area where the youth court and the ordinary adult court most differ. After all, at the trial stage, there is no difference between the two courts; the rules of evidence and the same principles of criminal law apply. But the magic of the youth court lies in its sentencing powers. The sentences, called dispositions, cover a wide range of options involving very little or no interference in the youth's life to radical interference. Sentencing a youth affects not only the youth, but the youth's family. It is a complex process.

The sentencing process for youths tends to be more "individualized" than it is for the adults. This is largely because the youth's "needs" feature prominently in sentencing. This individualized approach can in some instances result in longer or shorter sentences than an adult might get for the same offence. The public perception is often that youths "get away" with crimes and are treated too leniently. Although, because of a youth's inherent immaturity, the courts do from time to time act leniently, this is not always the case. In fact, many defence lawyers believe the opposite to be true; that is, that this "individualized" approach results, in many cases, in much longer sentences. This feeling is fuelled in large part by the fact that with respect to custodial dispositions youths do not have the advantages adults have, owing to the availability in the adult system of parole and "time off" for good behavior. For adults this can result in a substantial reduction of the sentence imposed. Youths, on the other hand, generally serve every day of the custodial disposition imposed. Moreover, since many of the youths who come before the youth court are troubled, and therefore have greater needs, greater intervention is often seen as justifiable. The sentencing judge will try not only to respond to the crime, but to the offender by trying to provide him with the type of environment that will assist in his proper development and growth.

Procedurally, both sides are given an opportunity to call witnesses and examine and cross-examine them. The youth, parents or guardians, social workers or any interested parties can testify to assist the court in making an appropriate decision. The youth can introduce any reports or documents that may assist the court in deciding what sentence is appropriate. If the parents, or guardians or other persons cannot be present at the sentencing and wish to be present, the court may, on request, put the matter over to another convenient date.

If the youth has no prior record of offences and the charge is not particularly serious, it is likely that sentencing will occur on the same day as the finding of guilt. Alternatively, if there is a prior record of offences, or if the charge is serious, the Crown attorney may request that a pre-disposition report be prepared. The time necessary for this varies with the locality, but in metropolitan areas, it will usually necessitate a three- to six-week adjournment, shorter if the youth is in custody, so that the probation office can prepare a report containing the background of the youth, the family and the offence.

This requires that the probation officer interview the youth, the family, police officers and other interested parties involved including the victim. The probation officer may, with the consent of the youth, review school reports or records, or prior reports done by other agencies, such as child protection agencies or treatment facilities. A copy of the report must be given to the youth, defence counsel, and the parents prior to the sentencing hearing. They will review the report to determine whether it is correct. Any amendments or corrections ought to be conveyed to the court at the time of the sentence hearing. The youth has the right on request to cross-examine or question the writer of the report.

According to the *Young Offenders Act*, as a general rule, a pre-disposition report *must* be obtained before a custodial term can be imposed. However, recent amendments to the Act provide for the imposition of a custodial term without requiring the pre-disposition report where both the Crown attorney and the defence agree to dispense with it. Where there is no consent, the Crown attorney may ask for a pre-disposition report when a custodial term is being sought, or when it is felt that a pre-disposition report would be of assistance in determining what sentence would be appropriate. The judge is not required to order the report, even when the Crown attorney requests it. If the judge feels a custodial term is not appropriate and there is already sufficient information before the court to make a decision, then the request may be refused. It is obvious that if such a report is ordered, the youth ought to cooperate and be of exemplary behavior between the date the report is ordered and the sentencing date.

Can a psychological assessment be obtained to assist in sentencing?
On occasion, a sentencing judge will be advised by defence counsel, parents or other concerned parties, that the youth is experiencing psychological problems that may require professional help. If the judge feels that the youth would benefit from a psychological assessment and that it is warranted by virtue of the circumstances of the offence, this can be ordered under section 13. According to this section, a judge may order the young person to be examined in order to assist the court in determining the appropriate sentence. This is usually done with the consent of the young person, but it can be ordered without that consent. These assessments are free of charge and generally require the cooperation of the family as well. While a youth can be placed in custody for an assessment, generally this can be achieved out of custody. The length of time varies, but it may take as long as four to six weeks for the assessment to be completed and a report to be before the court. Therefore, if this report is ordered, the youth will have to come back to court at a later date to be sentenced. By that time, the youth and parent will have read the report and advised the court of any inaccuracies. In the vast majority of cases, these reports do not reveal serious problems. Often referrals are made to a particular facility or program that will assist the youth and his family in their current difficulties. Sometimes the report will make direct recommendations as to a sentence that will incorporate the youth's needs. The judge is not bound to accept these recommendations although they carry considerable weight.

What sentences can be given to youths?
It is important to understand that sentencing options for youths are different than sentencing options for adults. Young offender sen-

tencing is governed by section 20 of the *Young Offenders Act*. Sentences for youths are called "dispositions" and vary from absolute discharges to custodial terms. These dispositions are limited in the sense that youths cannot be given a greater sentence than the maximum sentence that the legislation allows an adult to be given for the same offence.

When a youth court judge makes a disposition, the youth, defence counsel and parents are provided with a copy of a document indicating the sentence, and may on request, obtain a transcript of the reasons for sentencing.

How long can dispositions last?

This section refers to the maximum length of dispositions, so that youth court sentences can be seen in some perspective. Generally, dispositions cannot last for more than *two* years. The exceptions to this are prohibition orders and *custodial* orders which may last longer. This means that a youth cannot, for example, be placed on probation for over two years for one offence. However, if a youth is sentenced for different offences, the combined duration of the dispositions cannot, at the time of sentencing, exceed *three* years. Therefore, if a youth is being sentenced for two separate offences for example, theft of a car, and assault causing bodily harm, he can be placed on probation for a total of three years. In certain instances, dispositions for different offences are ordered to be consecutive or concurrent to each other or to a disposition already in force. For example, if the judge feels that twelve months probation is appropriate for two separate offences, he will indicate that the youth will be placed on probation for twelve months on the first charge, concurrent with the second charge. This means that the total probationary term is twelve months for both offences. As a result of recent amendments, combined dispositions longer than three years can be ordered when new offences are committed after the commencement, but before completion of any previous dispositions.

For example, if a youth on day 1, was placed on probation for a total of three years for a number of charges, and then on the following day was arrested and found guilty of another charge, the judge could place the youth on probation for a further two year term consecutive to the probationary term already in force. This would mean that the total probationary term would exceed three years, or here, would be five years. These dispositions can and often do extend beyond the youth's eighteenth birthday.

It should be noted that maximum dispositions are infrequently used and are generally reserved for the most serious offences.

What dispositions are available in youth court?
These dispositions can be made alone or, sometimes in combination with each other:

1. Absolute discharge
This is normally given to first offenders in matters that are relatively minor where no further punishment or supervision is required. For example, youths are often given an absolute discharge for stealing from a store, frequently called "shoplifting," where there is no prior record of offences. In effect, the finding of guilt is made and nothing more is done. An absolute discharge is granted according to paragraph 20(1)(a) of the *Act,* when it is in the "best interests of the young person and not contrary to the public interest." Despite its misleading name, a youth who receives an absolute discharge has still been found guilty of the offence and a youth court record is kept of that finding. If the youth is found guilty of another offence at a later date the court will be informed that the youth has already been granted a discharge. The judge will not likely grant another discharge on the second offence and will instead consider the other dispositions available.

2. Fines up to $1,000
This means that the court can require the youth, not the parents, to pay an amount of money as punishment for the crime. The judge generally inquires as to the ability of the youth to pay a fine and can consider the youth's present and *future* means. The judge will then determine what he believes is a reasonable amount, in all the circumstances, and grant sufficient time to pay. It would appear that a judge cannot order a youth to pay a fine and, in default, to serve a custodial term.

In provinces where work programs exist (called "fine option" programs), a youth who is required to pay a fine may discharge the fine by earning credits for work performed.

3. Compensation or restitution to injured parties
A youth can be ordered to pay compensation to another person "for loss of or damage to property, for loss of income or support or for special damages for personal injury arising from the commission of the offence where the value thereof is readily ascertainable." Therefore, for example, if a youth is found guilty of stealing $25 from his employer, the youth can be ordered to pay that amount back. This compensation can also be done by performing services for the person who suffered loss. Therefore, if the judge determines that in all the circumstances the youth in this example should work for his employer for free for a specified number of hours, and if the employer is agreeable, this can be ordered.

Further, if the youth acquired property during the commission of the offence, the property can be ordered returned to the owner. This is known as a restitution order. These orders can be made on their own or in combination with other dispositions. They are, for example, frequently combined with probation orders.

4. Community service order
Many jurisdictions have programs available to youths who are found guilty of offences and who are ordered by the courts, as a punishment, to do a specified number of hours of work without pay within a specified period of time, up to one year, for the community. The judge will make inquiries of the youth to see if this type of order is suitable, and will consider the youth's school and work commitments to determine the number of hours.

The youth who is ordered to do this work is told where to register. The youth is then assigned a particular job and a record is kept of the hours worked. The maximum number of hours is two hundred and forty. Where there are no approved programs, but where a particular person or organization has agreed to accept the youth, the court can still make an order under this section. For example, where a youth is found guilty of stealing a charitable donation box from his local store, he can, if the charitable organization is agreeable, be ordered to perform community service by doing work for that organization.

5. Prohibition, seizure or forfeiture
This provision refers generally to the power to require a youth *not*

to possess, or to forfeit, a certain item or items. For example, these orders are frequently used in the case of possession of weapons. The court may order that the youth forfeit the weapon in question and prohibit possession of any firearm or similar item for up to five years.

6. Detention for treatment
This provision allows a youth to be detained in a treatment facility for a specified period of time up to two years. This detention cannot be ordered without the consent of the young person, *the parents*, if they have maintained an interest in the proceedings, and the treatment facility. The prerequisite for utilizing this section is that a psychiatric report (ordered under section 13) recommends detention for treatment. This section is infrequently used because of the necessity for consents, and because the custodial alternative is also capable of providing treatment as required.

7. Probation
Generally, probation is imposed when it is felt that a youth could benefit from the supervision and guidance offered by probation services. Probation for one offence can last for up to two years. During or after the sentencing hearing the youth is advised of the conditions or terms listed in the probation order. He signs a form acknowledging this. A copy of the order is given to the youth and parent, if present.

There are two terms that are required to be in all probation orders. One requires the youth to attend court as required, the other requires the youth "to keep the peace and be of good behavior." This latter term requires the youth to stay out of trouble during the period of probation. It is considered an aggravating factor on sentencing when new offences are committed during a probationary term.

A frequent, but not required, term of probation is the reporting condition. When this is ordered, a probation officer is assigned to the youth and the youth is required to report to that person as indicated in the order. Often, the order does not specify precise reporting times, but simply states "report as required." In these circumstances, the probation officer, bearing in mind the needs of the youth, will set the dates and times for reporting. Reporting to a probation officer involves attending at the probation office for a discussion with the person assigned. These meetings can be very short or lengthy, depending on the youth's circumstances and the probation officer's availability. A youth should not wilfully miss these appointments because this can result in the youth being charged with the new offence of failing to comply with probation, which can result in the imposition of further punishment.

There are a number of other possible terms in probation orders, such as attending school or obtaining employment. Other reasonable terms can be included that will "secure the good conduct of the young person and prevent the commission by the young person of other offences." In practice, the probation order often contains some of the other dispositions. For example, it is very common to see an order of community service as an actual term of probation. As well, restitution and compensation orders are frequently terms of probation. Sometimes a court will order a youth to reside at a specific home or institution. This is done in some cases because these residences will give priority to youths only if a court directs or recommends the placement in a court order.

A youth can also be ordered, as a term of probation, to "reside in such place as the *provincial director* may specify." This section gives authority to the individual in charge of youth placements to require a youth to reside at specific premises and is often used to place a youth in what is in fact a custodial facility. Although the interpretation of this section is still in dispute, some judges utilizing this provision add the words "except in a place of open or secure custody." This is done because if a custodial facility is specified as the residence for a youth, this would circumvent the required considerations necessary before a custodial disposition can be imposed. With this possible exception, by virtue of this provision, a youth's residence can be controlled during the probationary period.

8. Custodial terms

As was stated earlier, a pre-disposition report is required before any custodial term is imposed unless there has been consent to dispense with it. This usually necessitates some delay between the finding of guilt and sentence. Before any custodial term can be imposed, the court must feel that it is

> ...necessary for the protection of society having regard to the seriousness of the offence and the circumstances in which it was committed and having regard to the needs and circumstances of the young person.

There are two levels of custody envisioned by the *Young Offenders Act*. The first level or open custody, generally means that youths serve their custodial terms in "a community residential centre, group home, child care institution or forest or wilderness camp." The second level of custody is reserved for youths who have committed more serious crimes or for youths with a prior record of offences. These facilities are locked and very strict controls are imposed. Each province designates certain facilities as either open or secure. A youth serving a custodial term must, subject to certain limited exceptions, be kept in a facility separate and apart from adults serving sentences. In either setting temporary absence or day release is available for a specific purpose such as education or employment.

When imposing a custodial term, the judge must indicate whether it is to be served in open or secure custody. The judge, however, cannot place a youth in a particular open or secure facility. That decision is made by the officials in charge of the facilities. The judge can, however, make *recommendations* concerning particular placements. Secure custodial orders can only be imposed in restricted circumstances. If the youth was under fourteen years when the offence occurred, secure custody can only be given for very serious crimes, that is, those that if an adult were charged would carry a maximum sentence of life imprisonment, or where the youth is charged with failure to comply with probation, being unlawfully at large, or escaping custody, or where a serious crime is charged in circumstances where the youth had been found guilty of a serious offence previously. If the youth is over fourteen years of age, then the conditions for obtaining secure custody are somewhat eased.

Custodial terms can be continuous, or intermittent. Intermittent terms are ones requiring the youth to serve the sentence at intervals, for example, on weekends or every other week. Each province may provide different facilities to accommodate this type of disposition. Prior to imposing an intermittent term the judge will require the Crown attorney to advise the court about the availability of placements for these dispositions.

As was indicated, youths cannot be given a greater sentence than adults are given for the same offence. This refers to the *maximum* sentence available for adults charged with the same offence. This provision is relevant mainly to custodial dispositions in the following circumstances: if the offence for which the youth is found guilty is dealt with summarily, or is a summary conviction offence, then the maximum custodial sentence that an adult can generally be given is six months. Therefore, a youth sentenced for a summary conviction offence can be given any of the full range of options available in section 20, but cannot be given more than six months in custody.

Subject to this exception, the maximum custodial term for one offence, in either an open or secure setting, is two years, unless the crime is one, that if an adult were charged, would be punishable by a maximum term of life imprisonment, in which case the maximum sentence is three years. For example, if a youth were sentenced for the crime of robbery, he could receive a maximum custodial disposition of three years because it is, for adults, punishable by a maximum sentence of life imprisonment.

The maximum custodial term that can be given for more than one offence is three years in total. Therefore, if a youth is being sentenced for a number of crimes, and the judge feels that he should impose a separate custodial term for each offence the total duration of the custodial terms cannot exceed three years.

Recent amendments allow for a duration of more than three years where an offence is committed after a disposition is imposed for a previous offence, and before that disposition is completed. For example, a youth is sentenced on day 1 to three years open custody for a number of offences, and on day 2 he escapes from the custodial facility. The judge dealing with the charge of escaping custody can sentence the youth to a consecutive term in custody that would in effect make the total duration exceed three years.

It should be noted that dispositions can run concurrently or consecutively. Frequently different charges arising out of a similar incident, or time frame, attract a concurrent term. Also, custodial dispositions can be made to apply concurrently where the total custodial term reflects a sentence that the judge feels is appropriate. Because of the distinction between open and secure custodial dispositions, when dealing with young offender matters a judge when sentencing for a subsequent offence can use concurrent terms in effect to change the level of custody from open to secure.

For example, a youth is sentenced to one month of open custody for car theft. After one week, he escapes and is caught and charged. On sentencing, the judge imposes a two-month concurrent term in secure custody. This has the effect of requiring the youth to serve the remaining three weeks for the offence of car theft and the additional five weeks for the offence of escaping custody in secure custody. According to recent amendments, the secure custody portion of consecutive terms of open and secure custody is served first. Therefore, if on day 1 a youth is sentenced to three months of open custody for certain offences and on day 4 he is sentenced to two months of secure custody on other offences, the youth will serve the two months of secure custody first.

As can be seen by some of the examples used, disobeying a custody order can result in the laying of further charges of escaping custody or being unlawfully at large. These offences are considered by the courts to be serious. As indicated, a youth, whether over or under fourteen years of age, can on sentence be ordered to serve a custodial term in secure custody if found guilty of these offences. Moreover, even if the sentencing judge does not impose a term of secure custody, the provincial director in charge of placements for young offenders may transfer the youth to a secure facility for a period up to fifteen days for these offences.

There is no parole or "time off" for good behavior in the young offender system. However, provision is made in the Act for temporary absence or day release. There is also the review procedure that allows a youth to apply to youth court to reduce a custody order or to change it from a secure placement to one of open custody. These provisions will be discussed at greater length at page 74.

9. Other reasonable conditions
This provision allows other conditions that are in the interest of

the youth and the public to be imposed. For example a youth can be ordered to pay money to charity or to write an essay explaining how the crime has harmed his family and society. This allows the judge more flexibility and creativity in sentencing.

What happens if a youth wilfully fails to comply with a noncustodial disposition?

Where a youth "wilfully fails or refuses to comply" with a youth court order to pay a fine, make compensation, restitution, perform a community service, obey a probationary term or other court order, a further charge can be laid. This offence originates in the *Young Offenders Act* and has been in effect since September 1, 1986. It is a summary offence. If the youth is found guilty, the sentence could include a custodial disposition for a term up to six months. Secure custody can only be given for this offence if it is based on a wilful breach of *probation*.

Chapter Eight

What Sentences Can Young Offenders Expect?

It must be emphasized that there is wide judicial discretion in the sentencing process. While the *Young Offenders Act* indicates the maximum sentences available, and provides sentencing options, it does not state what sentences are appropriate for what offences. Factors to be considered are the general principles of sentencing in criminal matters as indicated in case law or precedents, and the policy considerations provided in the *Young Offenders Act*, as interpreted by the courts.

1. Policy considerations
Section 3 of the *Young Offenders Act* seeks to balance the interests of the youth with those of society. The relevant factors considered in sentencing under this section are, on the one hand, that youths should "bear responsibility" for their offences and that society must be "protected" from crime; and on the other hand, that youths who commit offences have "special needs and require guidance," that youths have the "right to the least possible interference with freedom that is consistent with the protection of society, having regard to the needs of young persons and the interests of their families"; and that "young persons should be removed from parental supervision either partly or entirely only when measures that provide for continuing parental supervision are inappropriate." These latter factors can result in more lenient dispositions. They can also be used to justify more severe dispositions.

Also, when a custodial term is being considered, the *Young Offenders Act* indicates that custody must be "necessary for the protection of society having regard to the seriousness of the offence and the circumstances in which it was committed and having regard to the needs and circumstances of the young person.''

How these principles will be interpreted in each case will vary with the age and background of the youth, familial support, circumstances of the offence and the other sentencing factors to be considered.

2. General principles of sentencing in criminal matters

The basic goal of sentencing is the protection of the public. The public can be protected by removing the offender from society or by rehabilitating the offender. Clearly the best long-term protection that society can have is a rehabilitated offender. The question is, how can this be achieved? It is often said that the public is protected as well by the imposition of punishment which, because of its severity, deters others from committing crimes. The question is, should this factor affect the sentencing of young offenders, and if so, to what degree? The factors which are referrable to sentencing adults are not always directly applicable to young offenders.

The principles of sentencing are indicated in case law and can vary from province to province. As well, the application of these principles varies from court to court, with the result that sentencing law is complex. It is also constantly changing and evolving in response to public awareness and new social circumstances. Further uncertainty exists because the *Young Offenders Act* is relatively new and the sentencing factors for youths have not been fully enunciated. It is intended here to give just the basic rules that *may* apply in any given case.

Youthful first offenders are generally treated more leniently, and very often it is felt that the prime consideration is deterring the youth as opposed to deterring others. For minor crimes, therefore, first offenders are often granted absolute discharges. First offenders, however, who commit crimes of violence may well face a term of custody. Generally, before a custodial disposition is imposed, all other noncustodial options should be considered.

It is often said that in any consideration of the length of a custodial term, first sentences of custody should be short. Moreover, custodial terms ought not to be so long as to frustrate the prospects for rehabilitation. As well, a custodial term ought not to be unduly lengthened to "treat" the youth; rather the punishment should "fit the crime" and the offender.

There are aggravating and mitigating factors in sentencing. The aggravating factors include:

- the youth has a substantial prior record of offences
- the crime was committed while the youth was on probation
- the offence was planned and deliberate
- the youth was on bail for another offence when this offence was committed
- the crime involved a breach of a special duty or trust, such as when an employee steals from an employer
- there was substantial damage or injury done
- the youth has a psychological inclination towards this crime such that the chances that the crime will recur is high
- there has been a high incidence of these offences in the community, such as the rising numbers of thefts of purses from women
- a very negative pre-disposition report has been written indicating poor prospects for rehabilitation.

The mitigating factors include:

- the youth has no prior record of offences
- the youth shows genuine remorse for the offence
- the crime was not particularly serious, or was a spontaneous act
- a favorable pre-disposition report has been written concerning the youth
- the parents of the youth have punished the youth so that the courts need not do more
- the parents are very supportive of the youth
- the youth has been punished enough through the arrest process or pre-trial detention.

Too often it is said that youth's plea of guilty is a mitigating factor. It should be emphasized here that while a plea of guilty can be a mitigating factor as an indication of remorse, a plea of *not* guilty does not necessarily reveal a *lack* of remorse. Accused youths are entitled to a trial and the fact that they have exercised this right cannot be used against them on sentencing. Frequently it is said that a plea of guilty is a mitigating factor because the court has been saved the time and costs of a trial. While in some cases that may be considered a mitigating factor, the youth who chooses a trial should not receive greater punishment on sentence for doing so.

The interpretation of these factors, their application to a particular case and the weight to be given each factor, are matters for the judge to determine. As was stated earlier, sentencing is a very complex and difficult procedure. Perhaps it may be of assistance here to indicate *very generally* the kinds of sentences a youth can expect for specific offences.

Theft from a store, usually called "shoplifting," is an offence commonly committed by youths. First offenders frequently receive an absolute discharge or a fine or community service order. Other types of theft by first offenders rarely result in custodial terms. However, offences involving breaking and entering premises, robbery, arson, assault, including sexual assault, or weapons offences, even for first offenders, may well involve a custodial term. Youths with prior records of offences can expect the sentences for subsequent offences to increase in severity. Youths committing very serious crimes of violence, whether as first offenders or not, are frequently given secure custodial terms. Youths who have lengthy prior records of offences can expect to receive lengthy secure custodial terms for subsequent offences committed while on probation or shortly after being released from a prior term of custody, where it can be shown that all other dispositions have failed. Offences involving a breach of a court order, such as escaping custody, failing to comply with a bail order, or probation order, will often result in custodial dispositions.

What rights does a youth have if unsatisfied with the disposition imposed?

1. Sentence appeals
Youths have the same sentence appeal rights as adults. It should be noted that the Crown attorney can also appeal a sentence that he finds is not adequate. Generally a youth must file an appeal notice within a fixed period of time, often thirty days from the

date the sentence was imposed. A youth who appeals a custodial disposition can apply for bail while awaiting the appeal. A transcript of the sentencing hearing must be ordered because the appellate court will have to read that to determine whether there has been an error such that the sentence ought to be lowered. It may be that the *Young Offenders Act* does not provide for counsel as of right for the appeal, so that the youth will have to retain a private lawyer or apply to the local legal assistance programs for help. If the youth is unable to obtain a lawyer, an appeal can be launched without a lawyer. It is, however, obviously better to obtain the assistance of a lawyer on an appeal.

A youth will normally undertake an appeal when the disposition imposed is thought to be too harsh in all the circumstances. However, if the youth does not appeal, or does appeal and loses, the *Young Offenders Act* provides other opportunities to change a disposition or reduce the length of a custodial term where the youth has shown improvement.

2. The Review Procedure

Sections 28 to 32 inclusive provide a youth with a comprehensive means of reviewing or changing a disposition imposed by a youth court judge. It should be noted that a parent has the right to commence the review process as well. The *Young Offenders Act* grants all young persons the right to a lawyer, free of charge, at review proceedings. The youth court judge has the discretion to exclude the public from the courtroom during a review proceeding.

A. Reviews of custodial dispositions

1. Youth court reviews
Reviews of custodial dispositions can be requested by the youth at any time with the consent of the court, or as of right after six months. Moreover, where a custodial term or terms, totalling more than one year is imposed, there is a mandatory review of the disposition when one year has been served.

On a review, a youth court judge will consider a progress report compiled by the custodial authorities, and any other reports and testimony. The judge will consider all the circumstances, and "the needs of the young person and the interests of society" in arriving at an appropriate decision. A secure custodial order can be changed to one of open custody, or the custodial order can be changed to probation if the youth has shown sufficient progress. If the judge is not satisfied that the disposition should be changed, he will simply confirm it. It should be noted that a custodial disposition *cannot* be lengthened by this process, nor can an open custodial disposition be changed to one of secure custody.

2. Provincial director's recommendations

The person in charge of custodial placements is called the provincial director. If this person believes *at any time* that the needs of a youth serving a custodial term, and society's needs can best be served by placing the youth in an open setting, where the original disposition was for secure custody, or by releasing the youth from custody, and placing him on probation, then the matter can be brought before the youth courts. Once these recommendations are made to the court, the court may choose to accept them as it sees fit.

3. Review boards

These boards can be established by the province to carry out the review duties of youth courts, except that they cannot release a youth from custody. A youth can request that the review board change a particular placement either from one facility to another within the same level, or from a place of secure custody to one of open custody. The review board will hold a hearing in the same fashion as a youth court regarding this issue. A youth has the right to have any decision of the review board reviewed in youth court.

If a review board believes that a youth should be released from custody on probation, that recommendation can be made to the youth court. It appears that in the absence of further applications for review, the youth court is bound to follow the recommendation.

B. Reviews of noncustodial dispositions

A youth can at any time, with the consent of the court, or as of right after six months from the date the disposition was made, apply to the youth court for a review of a noncustodial disposition. A review may be requested because the circumstances leading to the disposition have changed, because the youth is having "serious difficulty" complying with the terms of the disposition, or because the terms of the disposition are inhibiting the youth's ability to take advantage of school, employment opportunities, and the like.

The judge on this type of review can confirm the disposition, terminate it, or vary it by, for example, giving the youth more time to complete it. It should be noted that the court *cannot* on this type of review impose a custodial term, nor can it without the young person's consent, impose a disposition that is "more onerous than the remaining portion of the disposition reviewed."

There is, apart from the review procedure, a general right to apply to the youth court for further time to complete a noncustodial disposition.

Chapter Nine

Some Other Matters

Does my child have a criminal record?
While records are kept of youth court proceedings, they are not made available to the public at large. Efforts have been made to make youth court documents confidential.

If a youth is acquitted, that is, found *not* guilty, all documents, photographs, fingerprints and other "records" referring to that charge are destroyed. If the youth is found guilty, or while the matter is pending, the youth court, police and some government departments keep records or documents concerning the youth.

These records are *not* disclosed to just *any* member of the public who wishes to see them. They can only be disclosed to persons listed in the Act who have a valid interest in seeing them, such as the accused youth, his defence counsel, the Crown attorney, parents of the youth or the judge. If a person not so listed wishes to see a document concerning a young person's charge, he must make an application to the youth court. The judge will allow a person to view a court document if he determines that there is a "valid interest in the record" and "if the disclosure is desirable in the interest of the proper administration of justice." The courts tend to interpret the confidentiality provisions strictly. On the basis of some decided cases, it is likely that immigration authorities, future employers, school personnel and other such individuals would have difficulty obtaining disclosure of these records.

When a youth is found guilty of an offence, those records are kept, but not indefinitely. The records can be destroyed five years after the date of the finding of guilt if the offence was a "summary" one, or five years from the date that the disposition is terminated if the offence was "indictable." Because of the difficulty in administering this section, the Act further states that when this five-year period is "realized" the records "shall be destroyed forthwith." At this time, the youth is "deemed *not* to have committed" the offence for which the records have been destroyed. Prior to destruction, but after this five-year period, the records cannot be made available to *anyone* except in very restricted circumstances, such as for statistical purposes or when a youth court judge allows it.

Subject to the provisions discussed above, a youth who is found guilty of an offence has a youth court record. If that youth is subsequently arrested for another offence or found guilty of another offence, that prior record will be before the court. Youth court records of offences are admissible in adult court (that is, for those over eighteen years of age) in the same manner as they are admissible in youth court.

What happens if another person encourages a youth to disobey a court order, or to commit an offence?

It is an offence under the *Young Offenders Act* to induce or assist a youth to disobey a condition of a disposition, custodial or non-custodial. This offence is tried in youth court and applies to both adults and youths. Any person who believes that this has occurred can refer the matter to the police.

Moreover, anyone who encourages, assists or counsels a young person (twelve to seventeen years of age) or a child (under twelve years of age) to commit a crime can be charged with the offence that the young person or child actually commits. This is so even where the child could not be charged under the *Young Offenders Act* because the Act, as was indicated, does not apply to those persons under twelve years of age.

Victims' rights in youth court

Victims of crime can generally be present at youth court proceedings and make their views and concerns known to the youth court judge. If a victim of crime cannot be present in court, but wishes to have his views presented, he can so advise the Crown attorney or police officer. Victims of crimes in youth court are interviewed where possible, when a pre-disposition report is made. When a youth is released on bail, a condition of release can be imposed requiring the youth to stay away from the victim. This can also be made a condition of probation on sentencing.

Also, on sentencing, a youth can be ordered to compensate the victim monetarily "for loss of or damage to property, for loss of income or support or for special damages for personal injury arising from the commission of the offence where the value is readily ascertainable." Where the victim consents, a youth can be ordered to compensate the person "by way of personal services." For example, where a youth deliberately breaks a window, and is thereafter found guilty of the offence of mischief to private property, a judge can, with the victim's consent, order the youth to wash the victim's windows once per week for three months. As well, if the young person has kept any property belonging to the victim, this can be ordered returned.

In trials involving sensitive matters, for example, sexual assault, victims of crime who are under eighteen years can, through the Crown attorney, ask the judge to exclude any member of the public from all or part of the proceedings. The judge will do so where he finds that the evidence given by the victim would be "seriously injurious or seriously prejudicial" and that the persons to be excluded are not "necessary to the conduct of the proceedings."

Also, the identity of a victim who is under the age of eighteen years is protected by the prohibition in the *Young Offenders Act* of the publication of his or her name or any information "serving to identify" him or her. Recent amendments to the Act would allow such a victim to apply to a youth court to *allow* publication of his own identity, if he wishes.

Chapter Ten

Sample Cases of Kids in Trouble

The scenarios described here are fictional. They are intended to illustrate some of the matters discussed so that they are more readily understandable. The outcome or decision by the judge in each scenario is also fictional and is not meant to convey that this would necessarily be the decision in that fact situation.

1. A "Reverse Onus" Bail Hearing
Mrs. B.'s daughter Susan is fifteen years of age. For about one year, Susan has been misbehaving at home by coming in after her curfew, not attending school, drinking alcohol and generally not obeying her mother.

One Saturday at about 1 A.M., Mrs. B. received a phone call from a police officer advising her that Susan had been arrested for theft of a package of cigarettes, (that is, theft under $1,000) and failing to comply with a condition of her previous release because she was outside her home after her 9 P.M. curfew.

Mrs. B. was somewhat relieved that Susan has been found. The officer told Mrs. B. that Susan would be held for a "show cause" or bail hearing on Monday morning. She said that this would be done because Susan was found guilty and placed on probation for theft some six months ago and that just one month ago she was arrested for theft and released on a recognizance with one surety, in the amount of $100, no deposit, with conditions that she obey a curfew of 9 P.M. each day. Now she had broken her curfew and allegedly committed another offence.

Mrs. B. agreed that Susan should be held in custody. She knew about Susan's prior arrests. Mrs. B. had been approved in court and signed as a surety on that last occasion, and since then things had not been going well. In fact, Mrs. B. was going to attend at the courthouse on Monday morning to withdraw her surety so that Susan would be arrested and taken into custody. The officer told Mrs. B. where Susan would be held over the weekend and what court she would attend on Monday morning. After Susan's arrest she was fingerprinted and photographed at the police station.

On Monday morning Mrs. B. went to the courthouse and spoke to the Crown attorney. She told her that she was not amenable to taking Susan home. Susan, who was in custody, requested to speak to the legal aid lawyer. She told him that she wanted to be released to her mother again, and that this time, she would do as she was told. The duty counsel told Susan that he had spoken to the Crown attorney and that she would not agree to release and was seeking a detention order. He told her that this meant that there would be a bail hearing and explained what that was and that it might be difficult to obtain bail because she had been on a release when she committed these new offences.

Court began and Susan's name was called. She was brought from the detention area, and the judge read the charges to her to ensure that she understood them. The Crown attorney then told the judge that Susan B. was in a "reverse onus" position and that the Crown was seeking a detention order. The legal aid lawyer indicated that he was content that the Crown attorney read the allegations to the court. The Crown attorney then read the written summary indicating what the police said that Susan had done. She also told the court of Susan's prior record indicating that she had been found guilty of theft under $1,000 some six months earlier and had been placed on probation for one year and that one month earlier she had been charged and released on a recognizance with conditions for theft under $1,000. She also told the court that Mrs. B. wished to testify for the Crown.

Mrs. B. then entered the witness box and was sworn. She told the court that Susan had been "out of control" for close to one year and that she felt that Susan should not come home at that time. She further indicated that Susan had broken all the conditions of her last release and that she did not want to change her behavior. Mrs. B. stated that she would not sign for Susan again and did not want her at home.

The defence counsel cross-examined Mrs. B. briefly. He suggested to her that this was the first time that Susan had been in custody and that this could have made a strong impression on her. Mrs. B. agreed that it was possible. He asked her if she would change her mind if Susan promised to change her ways. Mrs. B. stated that she would not. The Crown attorney told the judge that no further evidence would be called for the Crown.

The defence counsel then told the judge that he would be calling Susan to the stand to give evidence on her own behalf. Susan entered the witness box and the judge asked her if she understood her duty to tell the truth and knew what swearing on the Bible was. Susan stated that she did, and then she was allowed to swear on the Bible. The defence counsel asked Susan several questions about the difficulties she had been having and about the effect that detention had had on her. The Crown attorney then cross-examined Susan suggesting to her that she was promising to behave now so that she could be released, and not because she was sincere. Susan denied this.

No further witnesses were called for the defence and the judge asked both counsel for submissions. The defence counsel submitted that Susan should be released on her own undertaking with conditions. He indicated that the policy statements in the *Young Offenders Act* allowed "interference with freedom" only when the protection of society was an issue. He stated that her crimes were not such that this factor was applicable. He further submitted that this appeared to be more of a child welfare problem than a criminal problem and that Susan's sincerity about changing ought to persuade the court to order her release from detention. He told the court that a child protection agency was willing to take Susan and that she was in agreement with this.

The Crown attorney submitted that the onus was on Susan B. to persuade the court that she would obey any conditions of her release, if such was granted, and that if released she would engage in no further criminal activity. She submitted that Susan had not satisfied the onus on her and should therefore remain in detention. The Crown attorney went on to say that the youth had been both on probation and bail for the same offence when these offences occurred and that she had already promised the court to abide by conditions of release. She had broken that promise. The Crown attorney further stated that while protection of the public was a factor in denying freedom to youths, other factors were the needs of the youth and the interests of their families. Moreover, the Crown attorney indicated that in this case, continuing parental supervision did not appear to be appropriate. She went on to say that in view of the previous breach of release conditions, further release to a child protection agency was not appropriate.

The judge then made her decision. She indicated that Susan B. would be detained in custody pending her trial on these matters. She indicated that the reason Susan would be detained was that, in her view, Susan had not satisfied the onus on her that she would obey any conditions ordered by the court and not commit further offences. The judge went on to state that Susan was not being detained because she was "bad" at home or because her mother would not take her home, but because she continued to commit offences and had breached the previous court order of release.

2. A Plea of Guilty
Followed by a Crown Onus Bail Hearing

Louise A. had no problems at home or at school until she turned thirteen. At that time she began skipping classes and keeping the wrong company. She was caught shoplifting once and was given an absolute discharge in court. At fourteen years of age Louise left home. This occurred just after her parents had separated. She began living on the streets in the downtown core of the city. For about one month Mrs. A. had no contact with her daughter and did not know where she was.

Louise had some money on her when she left home. When this ran out, friends showed her how to make some easy money through prostitution. One night Louise was standing on the corner when a man pulled his car over to the curb in front of her. He rolled down the window and leaned over. She approached the car and asked the man if he "wanted a good time." He replied, "How much?" She indicated the price and when he agreed, she got into the car. Louise then directed the man to a laneway nearby. On the way there the man identified himself as a police officer and placed Louise under arrest for "communicating for the purpose of prostitution." He decided to hold her in custody for a bail hearing in order to obtain conditions that might prevent her from doing this kind of thing in the future.

Back at the police station, Louise gave the officer her mother's telephone number. The officer called Mrs. A., and advised her of the circumstances, and that Louise would be in court in the morning for a bail hearing. Mrs. A. indicated that she would attend court. Louise was held overnight in a young offender facility and brought to youth court the following morning. She spoke to the duty lawyer provided and decided that she would plead guilty to the charge and that she would not use the lawyer provided.

When Louise's name was called in court, she came forward and advised the judge that she wanted to plead guilty. The judge read the charge to her because it was her first appearance in court. He made sure that she understood the charge, her right to plead guilty or not guilty, and her right to have a lawyer represent her. She replied that she understood the charge and her rights. She stated that she did not want a lawyer to represent her. The judge inquired as to whether a parent was present. Mrs. A. stood up and identified herself to the judge.

The judge then read the charges to Louise and asked her how she wished to plead — guilty or not guilty. Louise replied, "Guilty." The judge then advised Louise to sit down and listen to what the Crown attorney read out.

The Crown attorney then read the facts to the court. Louise was asked whether they were correct and she replied "Yes." The judge then found her guilty of the charge and asked the Crown attorney whether there was a prior record of offences. The Crown attorney showed the piece of paper indicating the prior record to Louise and she agreed with it. The judge was then advised that Louise had been found guilty of theft one year ago and had received an absolute discharge. The judge then asked the Crown attorney what disposition she was seeking.

The Crown attorney stated that this was a very difficult case. She stated that the overriding principle of sentencing applicable to these circumstances was the "needs" of the youth under section 3 of the *Young Offenders Act*. She went on to state that a pre-disposition report or psychological report would be of assistance in determining the appropriate disposition for Louise.

At this point, Louise stood up and told the judge that she liked what she was doing and did not want any help. She said she just wanted to be left alone. Mrs. A., who had been crying quietly at the back of the courtroom, came forward. She begged the judge to "save" her daughter before it was too late. The judge asked Louise whether she was prepared to go home with her mother. She said, "Absolutely not."

The judge decided that a pre-disposition report was required. He inquired as to what the Crown's position was regarding Louise's release pending the completion of the report. The Crown attorney stated it was a Crown onus situation, in that there were no pending charges, and she would be requesting a detention order on both the primary and secondary grounds. The judge told Louise that she should use the free services of the duty lawyer to help her at the bail hearing. She refused.

Louise did, however, agree that the Crown attorney could read in the allegations made by the police. Since the facts were already known to the judge, the Crown attorney added that Louise had no fixed address for the last month and no means to support herself except through prostitution.

The judge asked Louise whether she wished to testify at the bail hearing and she said "No."

The judge asked for submissions. The Crown attorney indicated that Louise should be detained because there was no assurance that she would attend court, given her lack of roots in the community, and, in addition, in view of her inability to support herself, there was a likelihood that she would commit further offences, particularly prostitution related offences.

The judge asked Louise whether she would be willing to reside with a child protection agency if they would take her. She told the judge that she would run. The judge then made his decision. He told Louise that she would be released on a recognizance with one surety in the amount of $50. He indicated that Mrs. A. would be approved as the surety and that no deposit was required. He imposed further conditions of release requiring her to reside with her mother, to obey a curfew and to stay out of the downtown core of the city. He advised Louise that if she did not agree to those conditions or if her mother would not sign her out, she would remain in custody until the sentencing date.

The judge requested that the pre-disposition report be expedited in the circumstances and the case was adjourned for three weeks.

The duty lawyer explained what had happened to Mrs. A. She then went to the detention area to speak with her daughter. At first, Louise would not agree to go home with her mother. After about a week, she changed her mind and decided to give it a chance. After her release, both mother and daughter met with probation officers in order that the report could be completed.

When Mrs. A. and Louise returned to court, they were given the pre-disposition report to read. They agreed with its contents and discussed the matter with the duty lawyer. When Louise's name was called she came forward and agreed that the duty lawyer could speak for her. The Crown attorney indicated that in light of the week spent in custody and the positive pre-disposition report, a probationary term of one year was being suggested as a disposition in this matter. The duty lawyer agreed with this recommendation.

The judge told Louise that what she had done was more harmful to her than to anyone else in the community. He told her that she had not only hurt herself, but her mother as well. In imposing a period of probation he indicated that he agreed with both counsel and hoped that Louise would not be back in youth court.

3. A Plea of Guilty and a Noncustodial Disposition

Jean D. is twelve years of age. One day he and some friends, aged ten and nine years, were playing outside. Jean decided that it would be fun to see whether he could hit the bedroom window of the house next door with a rock. All three boys threw rocks at the window trying to break it but Jean threw the rock that ultimately broke it. The two other boys succeeded only in hitting and damaging the window frame.

The occupant of the house, Mrs. Perrone, was in her bedroom when this occurred. She looked out of the window and saw the boys with rocks in their hands. She knew who they were. She immediately called the police. The boys ran home when they realized that they might have been seen. The police arrived and after getting the addresses of the youths from Mrs. Perrone, they went to investigate the boys at their homes.

The police found out that the two boys with Jean were ten and nine years of age and therefore could not be charged with an offence under the *Young Offenders Act*. The police told the parents what had happened and warned the two boys. The police then attended at Jean's home. They told the parents that they had information that he had broken a window with a rock. The parents told the officers that they were aware of the circumstances because Mrs. Perone had called just moments earlier. The parents indicated their concern about Jean's behavior.

The police officers decided that a charge of mischief to private property would be laid, but that arrest was not necessary in the circumstances. Jean was given an appearance notice. The form required him to attend two weeks later to have his fingerprints and photograph taken and to attend in youth court three weeks later. Jean's parents were served with written notice of the date and place of this court appearance. They made sure that he had his fingerprints and photograph taken.

The police officers meanwhile had discovered that Jean had been warned before for the same thing. In fact, only two months ago, he had been part of the alternative measures program and as a result washed windows for twenty hours. The officers determined that this time the charge would have to be proceeded with in youth court.

On the court date, Jean and his parents attended together. They arrived early and were told that a legal aid lawyer would assist them if they wished. They spoke with her and showed her the receipt for $47.50 indicating that the damage to the window had been paid. The lawyer took down all the information and told Jean that he had the right to plead guilty or not guilty. The lawyer showed Jean the copy of the allegations that the police were making against him concerning the charge. He read these and agreed that they were correct.

When court opened, the Crown attorney began to call the names of accused from a list. When Jean's was called, he came forward in front of the judge. The duty counsel told the court that Jean had instructed her that he wished to plead guilty. The judge asked whether a parent was present. The duty counsel said that both were present and that the youth was twelve years old. Then the judge read the charge to Jean and asked if he understood it. He replied, "Yes, Your Honour." The judge then asked Jean if he knew that he had the right to plead guilty or not guilty. He replied that he realized that.

The clerk then read the charges to the youth and asked the Crown attorney how she elected to proceed. The Crown attorney elected "summarily." The youth was then asked how he wished to plead — guilty or not guilty. The youth stated, "Guilty." The judge then told Jean to be seated. The facts, as the police officer had recorded them, were then read by the Crown attorney and the judge asked the youth whether those facts were correct. Jean said that they were and the judge found him guilty. The judge then asked the Crown attorney whether there was a prior record of offences and was told that there was none.

The duty counsel then made submissions to sentence on behalf of the youth, indicating that he was quite sorry about this, had been punished at home, and had paid for the damage. She went on to say that as a first offender, the youth ought to be given an absolute discharge because a discharge would be in the youth's interest, and not contrary to society's interests.

At the end of the defence submissions, the Crown attorney made her submissions. She stated that she would be opposed to a discharge. She pointed out that the fact that the occupant was in her bedroom at the time the window was broken made it a dangerous act. She went on to say that some consequences should be imposed by the court to deter Jean and others from this conduct. After conferring with the duty counsel, she pointed out that Jean had already been part of the alternative measures program for the same offence two months earlier. The Crown attorney then submitted that a community service order ought to be imposed in the circumstances.

The judge then asked the parents whether they had anything to say. The father indicated that the boy was generally good and had responded well to the added chores given at home since the offence was committed. The judge then asked Jean if he had anything further to add. He said, "No."

The judge told Jean that he should respect other people's pronerty in the future, and that he should be a model for younger boys in the community, and not help them to do things that were wrong. She then told Jean that because of the fact that he had been good at home and had been punished by his parents, he ought to be treated more leniently than if this were not the case. The judge then inquired as to whether Jean got an allowance. On determining that he did, the judge ordered Jean to pay a $50 fine. She told him that *he* must pay the fine, not his parents. She also ordered him to write a letter of apology to the victim. The judge asked Jean how long he needed to pay the fine and was advised that it would take three months. She then gave him three months to pay the fine and to write the letter.

4. A Plea of Guilty and a Custodial Disposition

Ricky had been in the care of the local child protection agency for some five years. Over the past three years, he had been in and out of custodial facilities for various offences. He was currently serving an open custodial disposition of twelve months for breaking into and entering a house. He was placed in a group home with ten other youths and several staff. Although it was fairly easy to leave the house, the rules prohibited unauthorized departure.

Ricky was restless and decided this was not for him. One night, he opened the bedroom window and climbed out. He ran for a while and then slept in a park. Later he got hungry and decided to break into a house nearby to get some cash or food. He did so, but was seen inside the house by a neighbour and the police were called. He was caught in the house within minutes and arrested. On arrest, he gave the police a false name and date of birth.

After some hours, the police found out his real name and age. They discovered his record and circumstances and held him in detention for a bail hearing and gave notice to his guardians. He was fingerprinted and photographed. The police gave the Crown attorney the youth's prior record of offences and a summary of the current charges, which were breaking and entry and theft, escaping lawful custody and attempting to obstruct justice by giving a false name.

Just prior to the court hearing the following day, Ricky was told by the legal aid lawyer that he would have difficulty obtaining release from detention. They discussed the various options available and Ricky decided to plead guilty to the charges.

When Ricky's name was called in court, the legal aid lawyer told the court that Ricky wished to enter a plea of guilty. The judge asked Ricky if he knew what he was charged with, and because it was his first appearance, the charges were read to him. The judge then asked if a parent or guardian was present. He was told that a representative of the child protection agency was present. Ricky was then arraigned on all the charges. The Crown attorney elected to proceed by way of indictment on the charge of escaping lawful custody. (The break and enter and attempting to obstruct justice charges are indictable offences.) Ricky entered a plea of guilty to all the charges and after listening to the facts as read out by the Crown attorney, agreed that they were "substantially correct."

The judge then stated that he was satisfied that on the facts as read out, findings of guilt should be made. He asked the Crown if there was a prior record of offences. The Crown had already shown the piece of paper containing Ricky's prior record of offences to him. Ricky reviewed it with his lawyer and the Crown had been told that it was "admitted." The Crown attorney then handed the judge Ricky's record, indicating that it was admitted.

The Crown attorney asked the court to order a pre-disposition report in light of the serious nature of the offences and the background of the youth. The Crown attorney also indicated that he would be seeking a custodial term and that if the court felt that it was appropriate, a pre-disposition report would be required. The defence counsel indicated that she wished the report as well, and the judge agreed. Because the youth was in custody, the report was hastened, so that the youth was remanded to detention for three weeks for sentencing.

On the day set for sentencing, the report was read by all parties. The youth was asked if he agreed with the report and whether there were changes to be made to it. The youth indicated that it was correct. The report had recommended that the judge order compensation to the victim.

The judge asked the legal aid lawyer for submissions. She stated that the youth still had eight months to serve on his sentence (having served four months) in open custody. She asked the court to consider an open custodial disposition of perhaps thirty days consecutive to the existing disposition because the offences were spontaneous acts. She stated that Ricky did not appreciate the seriousness of his act and that the break-in occurred only because he was hungry. He then gave a false name because he panicked. She stated that Ricky had learned his lesson and he would not commit the same offence again. She further stated that he was intending to return to the group home the next day.

The Crown attorney then made his submissions. He indicated that break and enter is one of the most serious offences in the *Criminal Code*. If Ricky were an adult, he could face life imprisonment. Ricky was already serving a sentence for the same offence and had a lengthy record. He went on to state that the sentence for this offence must not only deter Ricky but other members of the community from committing such crimes.

The Crown attorney stated that the escape from custody and obstruction charges demonstrated Ricky's inability to cope with any freedom at all, and that the sentence should be two years in secure custody, concurrent to the existing sentence. The judge then learned that the child protection agency representative *and* group home director were present and wished to give evidence.

Each testified that Ricky had been making progress in that group home and that it was a good placement for him. They said that in their conversations with Ricky since his arrest, he had expressed the desire to return to the group home and stay this time. Each lawyer was given an opportunity to question these witnesses.

The judge considered all the submissions and testimony. He decided that Ricky should serve twelve months on each charge, concurrent, in secure custody. He indicated as well that the sentence should run concurrent to the sentence that Ricky was already serving. In his reasons for sentence, the judge pointed out that Ricky had not only left his custodial placement, but committed further serious offences. He stated that Ricky must be kept in secure custody for the protection of the public, given his lengthy record as well as the current charges. He added that Ricky's needs for strict controls could best be satisfied in a secure placement, and that if he showed progress, he could apply to the youth court for a review to change the disposition to an open custodial order or even probation.

Ricky was also placed on probation for twelve months following the custodial term, with the added condition that he report once per month to a probation officer.

5. A Plea of Guilty
Followed by a Psychological Assessment

Eduardo P. is a grade ten student. He lives with his parents in a good section of town. He has always done well in school and has never caused his parents any problems. Recently, however, he has become sullen and withdrawn over the loss of a girlfriend, Sheila.

On this day Eduardo left for school as usual, but he did not go there. Instead, he went to Sheila's high school to talk to her. She told him to "Get lost." Eduardo then waited until classes were finished for the day, entered the school and went to the area of Sheila's locker. He hid inside an empty classroom and waited. When he saw her she was alone, and he dragged her into the classroom. She screamed but he punched her until she stopped. He then sexually assaulted her. A teacher, hearing the screams, entered the classroom. Eduardo tried to run but was cornered. The police were called, and he was arrested for sexually assaulting Sheila and causing her bodily harm.

Eduardo was held by the police for a bail hearing primarily so that conditions could be obtained protecting the victim. The arresting officer called Mr. and Mrs. P. and advised them of the circumstances and where Eduardo would be taken for his bail hearing. He was photographed and fingerprinted and held overnight in a detention facility for youths. He was taken to court the next morning.

The duty lawyer saw Eduardo that morning. He later spoke to the Crown attorney to find out whether they could agree to release the youth. The Crown attorney told the duty lawyer that she could not agree with the police officer's recommendations for release, and would be seeking a detention order. The duty lawyer then spoke to Eduardo and his parents and prepared for the bail hearing.

At the bail hearing, the Crown attorney read in the summary of the facts as alleged by the police, and advised the judge that the youth had no prior record and no pending charges. The judge heard from the accused and his parents concerning the accused's ability to obey conditions that might be imposed by the court, and the parents' ability to supervise those conditions.

The judge asked for submissions. The Crown attorney indicated that the concern was for the secondary grounds; that is, the protection of the public. She stated that the alleged act was violent and unprovoked and occurred in a public school. The duty lawyer suggested that the public and the victim could be protected by releasing this youth on very strict conditions.

The judge decided that Eduardo would be released on a recognizance with one surety in the amount of $1,000 with no deposit required and with either parent approved. In addition, conditions were attached to the recognizance requiring Eduardo to stay away from Sheila and her school and to obey a curfew. The case was adjourned for three weeks to allow Eduardo to obtain a lawyer. Before Eduardo left the courtroom, the judge asked him if he wanted the charge read. He said no.

Eduardo and his parents returned to court on the specified date.

They had paid for their own lawyer who attended with them. The Crown attorney was advised by the defence lawyer that Eduardo wished to plead guilty to the charge. When his name was called, the defence lawyer told the judge Eduardo's intentions. He was arraigned and pleaded guilty. The Crown attorney read the summary of the facts to the court and Eduardo agreed that it was correct. The judge found him guilty of the charge.

The Crown attorney asked the judge to order a pre-disposition report and a psychological assessment to assist in determining the correct disposition. The defence lawyer opposed the request made by the Crown attorney. He indicated that the youth and the parents felt that Eduardo should be sentenced now and that in the circumstances a probationary term was appropriate.

The judge did not agree with the defence lawyer. He indicated that because a custodial term was possible, he had to order a pre-disposition report. In addition, he ruled that because the youth might be suffering from a psychological disorder, a psychological assessment was appropriate and would be of assistance on sentencing. He ordered that these reports be prepared. The youth was then required to return to court in six weeks' time to be sentenced.

On the return date Eduardo, his parents and his lawyer attended court. They read all the reports before entering the courtroom. When Eduardo's name was called the defence lawyer advised the judge that the youth and his parents had read the reports and that they were accurate. The lawyer went on to ask the judge to interpret the reports as positive, and Eduardo's offence as an isolated and emotional act, unlikely to be repeated. He stressed the point that in the nine weeks since Eduardo's release, there had been no further problems. He asked that Eduardo be placed on probation.

The Crown attorney indicated that Eduardo should be placed in open custody. She stated that while the reports disclosed that this behavior was an aberration, further counseling was recommended. The main consideration, she suggested, was the protection and safety of the community. She emphasized how important it is that schools remain safe. The Crown attorney further stated that the victim was still afraid of the youth and had suffered considerable physical and emotional trauma since the incident. She stated that while the victim was aware of her right to be present in court, she chose to not attend and chose rather to have the Crown advise the court of her concerns.

The judge decided that Eduardo should be placed in open custody for sixty days. He noted that Eduardo was a first offender and that he had spent one night in custody pending his bail hearing. He reviewed the reports and emphasized that while they were generally positive, they did reveal problem areas. He told Eduardo that resorting to violence is not a way to solve problems and that the courts will not tolerate violence in the schools. He was also placed on probation for two years with conditions that he have no contact with the victim and that he report to a probation officer once per month. The judge recommended that Eduardo seek counseling as indicated in the psychological report, but did not make this mandatory.

6. A Transfer Application Granted

Sandra is seventeen years of age. She has been living on her own, mostly "on the street" for about one year. Yesterday Sandra followed a young girl and caught up with her. Sandra told her to give up the shopping bags containing clothing that she was carrying. When the young girl refused, Sandra began punching her. A woman came to the assistance of the young girl. Sandra turned on her, took a knife out of her jacket and stabbed her several times. The woman fell to the ground. Sandra ran, but police caught up with her shortly. The woman was taken to hospital, where she was pronounced dead on arrival. Sandra was charged with first degree murder. After her arrest, she was brought to the police station by the arresting officers. Sandra was taken up to the investigative office. She told the officers her name and date of birth and then, having been apprised of her rights, told them nothing else. Sandra indicated, however, that she wished to call her lawyer to let her know about the charge and impending court appearance. She was given an opportunity to do so. Sandra was then fingerprinted and photographed.

Presently Sandra was taken to court for a bail hearing. Sandra's lawyer attended and the hearing began. Sandra's lawyer told the judge that Sandra knew what she was charged with and was prepared to give up her right to have the charge read. The Crown attorney called the police officer in charge of the case as a witness to tell the court of the circumstances of the offence and the accused's background. The court heard that Sandra had a long record going back five years, mostly for violence, that she had nowhere specific to live and had had no contact with her parents for about one year.

After cross-examination of this witness, the defence lawyer indicated that the defence would not be calling evidence. The Crown attorney asked for a detention order. The defence lawyer submitted that the offence was unfortunate, but not planned and therefore unlikely to recur, so that the youth should be released. The judge decided that Sandra should be detained in custody until her trial, because in all the circumstances, it would not be in the public's interest to release her. The matter was adjourned one week. At that time, the Crown attorney told the defence lawyer and the court that the Crown would be seeking to transfer Sandra's case to adult court. A date was then set, some four weeks away, for the transfer hearing. The Crown attorney also wanted an order to have Sandra examined psychologically, under section 13 of the *Young Offenders Act*. As well, the Crown attorney asked that a pre-disposition report be prepared. The request was granted by the court so that the reports could be considered on the transfer application.

At the transfer hearing, the defence lawyer asked for a non-publication order. This was granted. Thereafter, the Crown attorney called witnesses to indicate the psychological profile of the youth, her background, social history and future prospects and the ability of the youth court facilities and adult facilities to deal with her if found guilty. The defence lawyer cross-examined these witnesses and then called her witnesses. The defence witnesses indicated that Sandra could best be treated in the young offender system. The Crown attorney cross-examined the witnesses and then the judge asked for submissions.

The defence lawyer stated that the treatment resources for Sandra were available in the young offender system and not in the adult system. She further submitted that, while the offence was extremely serious, the three year maximum sentence provided by the *Young Offenders Act* could be seen as an adequate response to the offence in the circumstances.

The Crown attorney stated that Sandra was seventeen years

old and as such was almost an adult. She had a long record for crimes of violence and had had the advantage of the youth court treatment resources, but to no avail. She was alleged to have committed a very serious and senseless offence resulting in death. The Crown further submitted that the maximum sentence available in the *Young Offenders Act* was not adequate to deal with this offence or this offender.

The judge decided that Sandra ought to be transferred to the adult court because of her age and background and the seriousness of the offence. Sandra was upset and instructed her lawyer to appeal. This appeal was heard in the superior court but was dismissed.

In the meantime, Sandra was transferred to an adult jail and was brought before the adult court to set a date for a preliminary hearing.

7. A Trial in a Summary Matter

Danielle, Brad and Joan, all seventeen years of age, were arrested for possession of marijuana. They were taken to the police station and advised of their rights to remain silent, to obtain a lawyer and to have a parent or adult present. Danielle stated that she did not need a lawyer and that she wanted to make a statement because she was innocent. She signed a form indicating that she did not wish to have a parent or adult present during the taking of the statement. She also told the police officer that she understood her rights to consult with a lawyer and to remain silent. Danielle allowed the officer to type his questions and her answers. Then she read the statement over and signed it. In her statement, Danielle said that all she did was "pass a joint" and had never smoked it or had anything to do with it.

Brad and Joan, after giving the matter some thought, asked the police officer if he could suggest the name of a lawyer to whom they could speak. The officer brought out a list and provided the phone number of the first lawyer on the list. Brad called the lawyer and, when he got through, the officer left the room. Brad told the lawyer what had happened and the lawyer reminded him of his right to remain silent and recommended that he take advantage of that right. Brad decided to accept that advice. Joan felt that she should contact a different lawyer than Brad. After speaking to the lawyer, she similarly decided to not make a statement.

The officers, having been told of the situation, simply released Brad and Joan on promises to appear in court in two weeks and to appear for photographs and fingerprints in one week. When Danielle was finished making her statement, she was released as well on a promise to appear both in court and for photographs and fingerprints. All parents were notified in writing that their children had been charged with possession of marijuana and would have to attend court on a specified day. All the youths told their parents of the necessity of getting fingerprinted and photographed. Their parents accompanied them on the required day for this purpose.

On the date for court, Danielle's and Brad's parents attended but Joan's did not. They were all early enough so that they could get legal advice from the duty lawyer. After speaking with the lawyer, Joan decided to plead guilty. Brad and Danielle wished to have a trial. They were told how to go about getting a lawyer and that, because they were co-accused, it was best to get different lawyers.

Court began, and when their names were called, Joan told the judge that she wished to plead guilty. The judge asked whether the parents were present, and when he learned that they were not, decided that the matter should go over two weeks for the parents to attend. Brad and Danielle told the judge that they wished to put the matter over for two weeks to get a lawyer. The judge agreed and asked all three if they knew with what they were charged and read them the charge. They all left and returned in two weeks.

At that time, Joan attended with her mother. She arrived at the courthouse early enough to speak to the duty lawyer so that he could help her speak to the judge at the sentencing hearing. Brad arrived with his lawyer, and Danielle had a letter from her lawyer indicating dates for trial. When court began, their names were called. The judge was told that Danielle and Brad wished a trial date. Danielle handed her lawyer's letter to the Crown attorney, and Brad's lawyer let the court know when she was available. The Crown attorney checked to see when his witnesses were available. Soon they all arrived at an agreeable date some three months away. The two youths and their lawyers were then required to return on that date.

The duty counsel then told the judge that Joan wished to plead guilty and that her mother was present with her. After making sure Joan understood the charge and the meaning of a guilty plea, the judge had the charge read to her. The Crown attorney elected to proceed summarily and Joan pleaded guilty. The facts were then read out, and after agreeing with them, she was found guilty. The duty lawyer told the court that she had no prior record and that she was very sorry about this. He stated that she was experimenting with "pot" with friends. The Crown attorney stated that while she was a first offender, there must be a deterrent, so that a fine was required. The mother indicated that this kind of behavior was out of character for her daughter. The judge agreed and gave her an absolute discharge.

Brad and Danielle's trial date was approaching. About one month before the trial date, the defence lawyers for the two youths met with the Crown attorney to review the evidence that the Crown had. Danielle's lawyer saw the statement that Danielle had made to the police and told the Crown attorney that the Crown would not have to prove that it was voluntary. Brad's lawyer found out what the evidence was against Brad, and said nothing else.

On the trial date, Brad and Danielle attended with their lawyers and their parents. Their names were called and the charges were read to them. They both pleaded "not guilty." The Crown attorney called her first witness, the arresting officer, and asked him to tell the court what happened on the day that the accused were charged. He stated that when he entered the back room of the dance hall, acting on information received, Brad was holding a marijuana cigarette and Danielle was sitting next to him. With the consent of defence counsel, he then told the judge what Danielle said to him on arrest, (that is, her statement). Both lawyers then cross-examined the officer. Then the Crown called her final witness, an officer who indicated that the substance analyzed was marijuana. The defence lawyers again cross-examined the witness. The Crown attorney then told the judge that she was closing her case. The judge asked the defence lawyers what they wished to do.

Danielle's lawyer asked that there be an acquittal in her case because the Crown's evidence did not show her to have had possession of the marijuana as required by law. After hearing the submissions of the Crown attorney, the judge decided that there was no evidence against her, and dismissed the charge against Danielle.

Brad's lawyer indicated that Brad would be testifying and he entered the witness box. The lawyer asked Brad what happened that day and he told the judge that he never had any marijuana, but was only present when others were smoking it. The Crown attorney then cross-examined Brad, suggesting to him that he had just made up that story to be acquitted. No further defence witnesses were called, and Brad's lawyer asked the judge to give his evidence due consideration and find that there was a reasonable doubt as to his guilt. The Crown attorney asked the court to find that the police officers gave credible evidence and submitted that the charge had been proven beyond a reasonable doubt.

The judge decided that Brad should be given the benefit of the doubt and therefore acquitted him. In her reasons for the decision, she stated that there were a lot of people in that room and that the police officer on cross-examination admitted that it was dark, and that he had only a brief opportunity to see Brad. She found that he could have been mistaken, and that while Brad's presence there was suspicious, it could not be said that the Crown had proven his guilt beyond a reasonable doubt.

8. A Trial in an Indictable Matter

Ray was fifteen years old. He had just gotten out of custody and was living with his dad. He needed some "fast cash," and hung around the bus stop to watch for any women getting off the bus. Two women eventually did, and he followed the older one down a side street. He rushed up behind her and grabbed her purse. However, instead of freely letting it go, the woman held on to it. She lost her balance and fell over. Ray pulled harder, but he only succeeded in dragging the woman along the sidewalk. She was hurt and screaming. She hit her head on the curb and was knocked unconscious. A man working in his yard ran at Ray, who let go of the purse and ran. Ray was unable to get far; he was held for the police. He was arrested for robbery and taken to the police station. The woman was taken to the hospital for treatment.

At the police station, Ray was told of his right to remain silent, his right to consult with a parent or lawyer and to have either of them present during the taking of a statement. Ray told the police that he understood his rights, and did not wish to consult with anyone or have anyone present. Ray did call his lawyer to tell her that he would be in court later that day for a bail hearing. She told him that she would be there.

Some minutes later, Ray confessed to the police that he had been doing this sort of thing for the past week since his release from custody. He admitted that he did not always get a lot of money, but that the other day he had made some $80. The police found out that in fact several other women in Ray's neighborhood had been robbed recently.

The police asked Ray if he would make a written statement. Ray said he would, but that he wouldn't sign anything. The police proceeded to type the statement using Ray's own words. However, as he indicated, Ray refused to sign the forms stating that he had been advised of his rights and did not wish to consult with a parent or lawyer or have either of them present.

As a result of what Ray told the police, he was arrested and charged with two other counts of robbery in addition to the one for which he was originally arrested. The synopsis and background of the youth was prepared and provided to the Crown attorney. Ray's fingerprints and photograph were taken. Ray was then taken to the courthouse (court was still in progress) for a bail hearing.

At the bail hearing, Ray appeared with his lawyer. The Crown attorney indicated that she was seeking a detention order, and the judge after hearing all the facts and testimony, imposed a detention order. The judge stated, "Ray's lengthy record and these serious allegations mean that it would not be in the public's interests to release him." Defence counsel indicated that she was prepared to set a trial date. Because Ray was in detention, a date some four weeks away was set.

On the trial date, Ray's lawyer told the Crown attorney that she would be contesting the admissibility of the statement made by Ray after his arrest. The Crown attorney indicated that she would not be trying to admit the statement into evidence because the "waiver" of rights form had not been signed by Ray as required by the *Young Offenders Act*. The Crown attorney told the defence counsel that she would be relying on the testimony of the victims and the witness only.

In court, Ray's name was called. The judge found out that Ray's father was present in court and that Ray had a lawyer. The charges were read to him and he was asked whether he wished to plead guilty or not guilty. Ray pleaded "not guilty." The defence lawyer asked for an order excluding all witnesses. The judge granted the order and all the witnesses left the courtroom and waited outside until their names were called. Ray, of course, remained in the courtroom throughout.

The first witness was the elderly woman whom, it was alleged, Ray had dragged along the sidewalk. She took the witness stand and promised to tell the truth by "affirmation." She is eighty years of age.

The Crown attorney asked her to tell the court what happened. The lady told her story indicating that she "didn't know what hit her." She stated that suddenly she was being dragged along the sidewalk and that she had held on to her purse as a reflex action. Her purse contained $30 and the boy did not get it.

She indicated that she had physical injuries after the attack — a fractured hip, mild concussion and cuts and bruises. She stated that now she was afraid to walk on the street. The Crown attorney asked her if she saw the person in court who had done this to her. She looked around and stated that it had happened too fast, and that she could not identify the person. The defence lawyer told the judge that she had no questions to ask of this witness. The witness was then told by the judge that she was free to leave.

The Crown attorney had the next witness paged outside the courtroom. He entered, took the stand and swore on the Bible to tell the truth. He indicated that he had happened to be working in his yard when he heard screams. He identified the accused youth as the boy whom he saw pulling at the lady's purse. He said he had pursued the youth and caught and held him for the police. He stated that a small crowd had gathered and that people were attending to the elderly woman. The police and ambulance had arrived within minutes.

In cross-examination, the defence lawyer suggested to the witness that what he really had seen was a boy running in close proximity to a woman who was screaming and lying on the ground. The witness denied this. He insisted that he had seen the boy tugging at the woman's purse.

The Crown attorney called the next witness. She was a middle aged woman who preferred to give her evidence through the

Cantonese interpreter provided by the Court. After being sworn, she related how two days before the incident involving the elderly woman, her purse had been snatched by a young boy. She pointed to the accused and stated, through the interpreter, "That's the one; I'll never forget his face." She indicated that on returning from the bank with about $80 in cash in her wallet, a young boy had come at her from behind and grabbed her purse from under her arm and run. She had just enough time to see his face for an instant.

The defence lawyer asked the woman to describe the boy. The woman stated that she had not had time to take notes — "It happened so quickly." The lawyer suggested to the witness that she was really only guessing that the accused was the boy who had done this. The witness denied this.

The Crown attorney then called her final witness. The young woman entered the courtroom and took the stand. She swore on the Bible to tell the truth and in response to the Crown attorney's question, related what happened to her: "I was walking along the street from the grocery store when a boy walking towards me grabbed my purse off my shoulder. I thought, what nerve! So I chased him, screaming and yelling. He kept looking back to see where I was and ran into a bicycle chained to a pole. I reached him and tried to pin him to the ground. I was about six inches from his face. Suddenly he threw me off and ran away. I fell over on the sidewalk and lost sight of him. Then I called the police."

The Crown attorney asked the woman if she could identify any one in court as being that boy. The woman pointed to the accused and stated that she was absolutely certain that he was the one.

The defence counsel asked the woman to describe the boy who had attacked her. The witness gave a lengthy and detailed description. The defence lawyer suggested that she could not have seen the youth's face for very long. The witness denied this. The defence lawyer tried unsuccessfully to discredit this witness's identification. The witness stood firm.

The Crown attorney told the court that no further witnesses would be called for the Crown. The judge asked the defence lawyer if she would be calling evidence. She indicated that she would not, and the judge then asked both lawyers for submissions.

The Crown attorney stated that all three charges of robbery had been proven beyond a reasonable doubt. She stated that the youth was positively identified in two cases and in the third was caught right after.

The defence lawyer argued that the identification evidence was too weak on all the charges to amount to proof in a criminal trial. She told the court of a number of precedents that supported her point of view.

The judge stated that Ray would be found guilty on the first charge involving the elderly woman and the third charge involving the young woman. He stated that he was not satisfied with the quality of the identification in the second charge. He went on to state that the evidence of the witness who caught Ray was not shaken in cross-examination and was direct evidence proving Ray's guilt on that charge. With respect to the third charge, the woman had had a good opportunity to see the accused and was sure that it was the accused. The judge indicated that, in weighing all the evidence, he was satisfied beyond a reasonable doubt and made findings of guilt on the two charges.

The judge then asked the Crown attorney whether there was a prior record of offences. The Crown showed the paper containing the record to defence counsel who, after reviewing it with her client, admitted that it was correct. The judge then reviewed the record and asked both lawyers for sentencing submissions.

Both lawyers agreed to dispense with the requirements of ordering a pre-disposition report because a previous report, which was shown to the judge, had been done only two months ago. The Crown attorney stated that she was seeking the maximum sentence of three years secure custody on these charges. She indicated that women were being victimized by youths like Ray and that the sentence should reflect society's abhorrence for this conduct. Moreover, she stated that the sentence ought to be long enough to deter him and others from doing this in the future. After reviewing the facts, the Crown attorney urged the judge to impose a sentence that would protect innocent citizens on public streets.

The defence lawyer stated that Ray had been in custody for about one month awaiting his trial and that this should be considered. She reviewed the policy statements listed in the *Young Offenders Act* and asked the judge to consider Ray's deprived background and prospects for rehabilitation. She stated that at fifteen years of age, a three-year sentence might crush him and frustrate any attempts at changing him. She submitted that a sentence in the range of three months in open custody would be a significant sentence that would deter him and others from engaging in this sort of thing in the future.

The judge decided to impose the maximum sentence of three years in secure custody, concurrent on each charge. He stated that these crimes were despicable and cowardly and had to be stopped. He pointed out that real and serious injury occurred to one of these women and that it was the result of the deliberate act of the youth. He referred to the *Young Offenders Act* and the fact that the protection of the public was indicated as a factor in sentencing as well as the needs of the youth and the interests of his family. The judge indicated that it was apparent to him that long-term treatment and care was necessary before Ray could be rehabilitated. He also cited the review positions of the *Young Offenders Act* which provide for opportunities for lowering or changing the secure disposition if there is improvement.

Chapter Eleven

Last Words

At first glance, it may appear from all the rules and provisions discussed that the legal system regarding young offenders is formal. It is difficult in a book of this nature to describe these procedures and rules and still to convey the flexibility of the law. The law, however, has the dubious distinction of having to be both formal and flexible. It must, for example, be formal when defending the rights of individuals. Indeed, the vast majority of the rules discussed act as safeguards to ensure that youths are treated fairly and are made aware of their rights. Viewed as a whole, these safeguards or protections given to youths are reasonable in light of the serious consequences that can follow from a finding of guilt.

It may appear from some of these rules, particularly the rule ensuring the accused youth's right to remain silent and the rule requiring the Crown attorney to prove the guilt of the accused youth beyond a reasonable doubt, that accused youths, who are in fact guilty, can and do get acquitted. This may be true, but it is also a basic principle of the criminal justice system that it is preferable that some guilty go free than that an innocent person be found guilty. Many of the rules exist to preclude the innocent from that very fate.

The juvenile justice system is in many ways, despite the number of rules, a flexible and humane system. There are many areas where judicial and tactical discretion can be exercised. There is, as well, a comprehensive appeal procedure to ensure that youths are dealt with fairly and according to the law. On sentence, in addition to the appeal process, youths can take advantage of the many avenues for dispositional review. This ensures that post-sentence effort and accomplishment can be rewarded. Indeed, sentencing options in youth court are varied and flexible enough so that the disposition can respond not only to the crime, but to the offender's needs as well.

It may be encouraging for the parents of the youths who do get into trouble to know that the majority of these youths do not become repeat offenders. The experience of arrest and the effect of being brought before the youth court is usually enough to deter them from further crime. Moreover, the confidentiality of the "records" in youth court goes a long way to ensure that a finding of guilt does not damage a youth's future and impair his ability to go on to become a productive citizen.

It may also be of assistance to try, even briefly, to answer the question *why do kids get into trouble?* It is beyond both the scope of this book and my expertise to give an adequate response to this difficult question. It may suffice for these purposes to say there are many reasons. Sometimes the offence can be explained simply by immaturity, or it may be a spontaneous act, or the youth may have been motivated or led by others. There are many factors both inside and outside the home that influence a youth's behavior. Clearly it is too simplistic to blame parents for the crimes committed by their children. Unfortunately it is the case that youths from all kinds of backgrounds — good and bad — are found guilty of offences before the youth court.

Many rules and procedures have been discussed. Just as many, if not more, have been omitted. Value judgments as to what was important and helpful and what was not, had to be made. It is hoped that the objectives of this book have been fulfilled and the matters discussed have provided the reader with a practical guide to youth court proceedings.

Appendix A
YOUNG OFFENDERS ACT
S.C. 1980-81-82-83, *c.* 110, *as amended.*

1. This Act may be cited as the *Young Offenders Act*. Short title

Interpretation
2. (1) In this Act, Definitions
(a) "adult" means a person who is neither a young person nor a child; Adult
(b) "alternative measures" means measures other than judicial proceedings under this Act used to deal with a young person alleged to have committed an offence; Alternative measures
(c) "child" means a person who is or, in the absence of evidence to the contrary, appears to be under the age of twelve years; Child
(d) "disposition" means a disposition made under section 20 or sections 28 to 32 and includes a confirmation or a variation of a disposition; Disposition
(e) "offence" means an offence created by an Act of Parliament or by any regulation, rule, order, by-law or ordinance made thereunder other than an ordinance of the Yukon Territory or the Northwest Territories; Offence
(f) "ordinary court" means the court that would, but for this Act, have jurisdiction in respect of an offence alleged to have been committed; Ordinary court
(g) "parent" includes, in respect of another person, any person who is under a legal duty to provide for that other person or any person who has, in law or in fact, the custody or control of that other person but does not include a person who has the custody or control of that other person by reason only of proceedings under this Act; Parent
(h) "predisposition report" means a report on the personal and family history and present environment of a young person made in accordance with section 14; Predisposition report
(i) "progress report" means a report made in accordance with section 28 on the performance of a young person against whom a disposition has been made; Progress report
(j) "provincial director" means a person, a group or class of persons or a body appointed or designated by or pursuant to an Act of the Provincial director

legislature of a province or by the Lieutenant Governor in Council of a province or his delegate to perform in that province, either generally or in a specific case, any of the duties or functions of a provincial director under this Act;

Review board

(k) "review board" means a review board established or designated by a province for the purposes of section 30;

Young person

(l) "young person" means a person who is or, in the absence of evidence to the contrary, appears to be
  (i) twelve years of age or more, but
  (ii) under eighteen years of age or, in a province in respect of which a proclamation has been issued under subsection (2) prior to April 1, 1985, under sixteen or seventeen years, whichever age is specified by the proclamation,
and, where the context requires, includes any person, who is charged under this Act with having committed an offence while he was a young person or is found guilty of an offence under this Act;

Youth court

(m) "youth court" means a court established or designated by or under an Act of the legislature of a province, or designated by the Governor in Council or the Lieutenant Governor in Council of a province, as a youth court for the purposes of this Act;

Youth court judge

(n) "youth court judge" means a person appointed to be a judge of a youth court;

Youth worker

(o) "youth worker" means a person appointed or designated, whether by title of youth worker or probation officer or by any other title, by or pursuant to an Act of the legislature of a province or by the Lieutenant Governor in Council of a province or his delegate, to perform, either generally or in a specific case, in that province any of the duties or functions of a youth worker under this Act. 1986, c. 32, s. 1.

Proclamation changing definition of "young person"

(2) The Governor in Council may, at any time prior to April 1, 1985, by proclamation
  (a) direct that in any province "young person", for the purposes of this Act, means a person who is or, in the absence of evidence to the contrary, appears to be twelve years of age or more, but under sixteen or under seventeen years of age, as the case may be; and
  (b) revoke any direction made under paragraph (a).

Limitation

(3) Any direction made under paragraph (2) (a) shall cease to have effect on April 1, 1985.

(4) Unless otherwise provided, words and expressions used in this Act have the same meaning as in the *Criminal Code*. 1986, c. 32, s. 1.

Words and expressions

2.1. Any power, duty or function of a provincial director under this Act may be exercised or performed by any person authorized by the provincial director to do so and, if so exercised or performed, shall be deemed to have been exercised or performed by the provincial director. 1986, c. 32, s. 2.

Powers, duties and functions of provincial directors

Declaration of Principle

3. (1) It is hereby recognized and declared that
(a) while young persons should not in all instances be held accountable in the same manner or suffer the same consequences for their behaviour as adults, young persons who commit offences should nonetheless bear responsibility for their contraventions;
(b) society must, although it has the responsibility to take reasonable measures to prevent criminal conduct by young persons, be afforded the necessary protection from illegal behaviour;
(c) young persons who commit offences require supervision, discipline and control, but, because of their state of dependency and level of development and maturity, they also have special needs and require guidance and assistance;
(d) where it is not inconsistent with the protection of society, taking no measures or taking measures other than judicial proceedings under this Act should be considered for dealing with young persons who have committed offences;
(e) young persons have rights and freedoms in their own right, including those stated in the *Canadian Charter of Rights and Freedoms* or in the *Canadian Bill of Rights*, and in particular a right to be heard in the course of, and to participate in, the processes that lead to decisions that affect them, and young persons should have special guarantees of their rights and freedoms;
(f) in the application of this Act, the rights and freedoms of young persons include a right to the least possible interference with freedom that is consistent with the protection of society, having regard to the needs of young persons and the interests of their families;
(g) young persons have the right, in every instance where they have rights or freedoms that may be affected by this Act, to be informed as to what those rights and freedoms are; and
(h) parents have responsibility for the care and supervision of their children, and, for that reason,

Policy for Canada with respect to young offenders

young persons should be removed from parental supervision either partly or entirely only when measures that provide for continuing parental supervision are inappropriate.

Act to be liberally construed

(2) This act shall be liberally construed to the end that young persons will be dealt with in accordance with the principles set out in subsection (1).

Alternative Measures

Alternative measures

4. (1) Alternative measures may be used to deal with a young person alleged to have committed an offence instead of judicial proceedings under this Act only if
  (a) the measures are part of a program of alternative measures authorized by the Attorney General or his delegate or authorized by a person, or a person within a class of persons, designated by the Lieutenant Governor in Council of a province;
  (b) the person who is considering whether to use such measures is satisfied that they would be appropriate, having regard to the needs of the young person and the interests of society;
  (c) the young person, having been informed of the alternative measures, fully and freely consents to participate therein;
  (d) the young person has, before consenting to participate in the alternative measures, been advised of his right to be represented by counsel and been given a reasonable opportunity to consult with counsel;
  (e) the young person accepts responsibility for the act or omission that forms the basis of the offence that he is alleged to have committed;
  (f) there is, in the opinion of the Attorney General or his agent, sufficient evidence to proceed with the prosecution of the offence; and
  (g) the prosecution of the offence is not in any way barred at law.

Restriction on use

(2) Alternative measures shall not be used to deal with a young person alleged to have committed an offence if the young person
  (a) denies his participation or involvement in the commission of the offence; or
  (b) expresses his wish to have any charge against him dealt with by the youth court.

Admissions not admissible in evidence

(3) No admission, confession or statement accepting responsibility for a given act or omission made by a young person alleged to have committed an offence as a condition of his being dealt with by alternative measures shall be admissible in evidence against him in any civil or criminal proceedings.

No bar to proceedings

(4) The use of alternative measures in respect of a young

person alleged to have committed an offence is not a bar to proceedings against him under this Act, but
  (a) where the youth court is satisfied on a balance of probabilities that the young person has totally complied with the terms and conditions of the alternative measures, the youth court shall dismiss any charge against him; and
  (b) where the youth court is satisfied on a balance of probabilities that the young person has partially complied with the terms and conditions of the alternative measures, the youth court may dismiss any charge against him if, in the opinion of the court, the prosecution of the charge would, having regard to the circumstances, be unfair, and the youth court may consider the young person's performance with respect to the alternative measures before making a disposition under this Act.

(5) Subject to subsection (4), nothing in this section shall be construed to prevent any person from laying an information, obtaining the issue or confirmation of any process or proceeding with the prosecution of any offence in accordance with law. — Laying of information, etc.

Jurisdiction

5. (1) Notwithstanding any other Act of Parliament but subject to the *National Defence Act* and section 16, a youth court has exclusive jurisdiction in respect of any offence alleged to have been committed by a person while he was a young person and any such person shall be dealt with as provided in this Act. — Exclusive jurisdiction of youth court; Period of limitation

(2) No proceedings in respect of an offence shall be commenced under this Act after the expiration of the time limit set out in any other Act of Parliament or any regulation made thereunder for the institution of proceedings in respect of that offence. — Proceedings continued when adult

(3) Proceedings commenced under this Act against a young person may be continued, after he becomes an adult, in all respects as if he remained a young person. — Powers of youth court judge

(4) A youth court judge, for the purpose of carrying out the provisions of this Act, is a justice and a provincial court judge and has the jurisdiction and powers of a summary conviction court under the *Criminal Code*. 1986, c. 32, s. 3. — Court of record

(5) A youth court is a court of record. 1986, c. 32, s. 3.

6. Any proceeding that may be carried out before a justice under the *Criminal Code*, other than a plea, a trial or an adjudication, may be carried out before such justice in respect of an offence alleged to have been committed by a young person, and any process that may be issued by a justice under the *Criminal Code* may be issued by such — Certain proceedings may be taken before justices justice in respect of an offence alleged to have been committed by a young person. 1986, c. 32, s. 4.

Detention Prior to Disposition

7. (1) A young person who is

- (a) arrested and detained prior to the making of a disposition in respect of the young person under section 20, or
- (b) detained pursuant to a warrant issued under subsection 32(6)

shall, subject to subsection (4), be detained in a place of temporary detention designated as such by the Lieutenant Governor in Council of the appropriate province or his delegate or in a place within a class of such places so designated.

(1.1) A young person who is detained in a place of temporary detention pursuant to subsection (1) may, in the course of being transferred from that place to the court or from the court to that place, be held under the supervision and control of a peace officer.

(2) A young person referred to in subsection (1) shall be held separate and apart from any adult who is detained or held in custody unless a youth court judge or a justice is satisfied that

- (a) the young person cannot, having regard to his own safety or the safety of others, be detained in a place of detention for young persons; or
- (b) no place of detention for young persons is available within a reasonable distance.

(3) A young person who is detained in custody in accordance with subsection (1) may, during the period of detention, be transferred by the provincial director from one place of temporary detention to another.

(4) Subsections (1) and (2) do not apply in respect of any temporary restraint of a young person under the supervision and control of a peace officer after arrest, but a young person who is so restrained shall be transferred to a place of temporary detention referred to in subsection (1) as soon as is reasonably practicable, and in no case later than the first reasonable opportunity after the appearance of the young person before a youth court judge or a justice pursuant to section 454 of the *Criminal Code*.

(5) In any province for which the Lieutenant Governor in Council has designated a person or a group of persons whose authorization is required, either in all circumstances or in circumstances specified by the Lieutenant Governor in Council, before a young person who has been arrested may be detained in accordance with this section, no young person shall be so detained unless the authorization is obtained.

(6) *Determination by provincial authority of place of detention* In any province for which the Lieutenant Governor in Council has designated a person or a group of persons who may determine the place where a young person who has been arrested may be detained in accordance with this section, no young person may be so detained in a place other than the one so determined. 1986, c. 32, s. 5. Determination by provincial authority of place of detention

7.1. (1) Where a youth court judge or a justice is satisfied that Placement of young persons in care of responsible person
  (a) a young person who has been arrested would, but for this subsection, be detained in custody,
  (b) a responsible person is willing and able to take care of and exercise control over the young person, and
  (c) the young person is willing to be placed in the care of that person,
the young person may be placed in the care of that person instead of being detained in custody.

(2) A young person shall not be placed in the care of a person under subsection (1) unless Condition of placement
  (a) that person undertakes in writing to take care of and to be responsible for the attendance of the young person in court when required and to comply with such other conditions as the youth court judge or justice may specify; and
  (b) the young person undertakes in writing to comply with the arrangement and to comply with such other conditions as the youth court judge or justice may specify.

(3) Where a young person has been placed in the care of a person under subsection (1) and Removing young person from care
  (a) that person is no longer willing or able to take care of or exercise control over the young person, or
  (b) it is, for any other reason, no longer appropriate that the young person be placed in the care of that person,
the young person, the person in whose care the young person has been placed or any other person may, by application in writing to a youth court judge or a justice, apply for an order under subsection (4).

(4) Where a youth court judge or a justice is satisfied that a young person should not remain in the custody of the person in whose care he was placed under subsection (1), the youth court judge or justice shall Order
  (a) make an order relieving the person and the young person of the obligations undertaken pursuant to subsection (2), and
  (b) issue a warrant for the arrest of the young person.

(5) Where a young person is arrested pursuant to a warrant Effect of arrest

issued under paragraph (4)(b), the young person shall be taken before a youth court judge or justice forthwith and dealt with under section 457 of the *Criminal Code*. 1986, c. 32, s. 5.

Offence and punishment

7.2. Any person who wilfully fails to comply with section 7, or with an undertaking entered into pursuant to subsection 7.1(2), is guilty of an offence punishable on summary conviction. 1986, c. 32, s. 5.

Order respecting detention or release

8. (1) Repealed. 1986, c. 32, s. 6, effective September 1, 1986.

Application to youth court

(2) Where an order is made under section 457 of the *Criminal Code* in respect of a young person by a justice who is not a youth court judge, an application may, at any time after the order is made, be made to a youth court for the release from or detention in custody of the young person, as the case may be, and the youth court shall hear the matter as an original application.

Notice to prosecutor

(3) An application under subsection (2) for release from custody shall not be heard unless the young person has given the prosecutor at least two clear days' notice in writing of the application.

Notice to young person

(4) An application under subsection (2) for detention in custody shall not be heard unless the prosecutor has given the young person at least two clear days' notice in writing of the application.

Waiver of notice

(5) The requirement for a notice under subsection (3) or (4) may be waived by the prosecutor or by the young person or his counsel, as the case may be.

Application for review under section 457.5 or 457.6 of Criminal Code

(6) An application under section 457.5 or 457.6 of the *Criminal Code* for a review of an order made in respect of a young person by a youth court judge who is a judge of a superior, county or district court shall be made to a judge of the court of appeal.

Idem

(7) No application may be made under section 457.5 or 457.6 of the *Criminal Code* for a review of an order made in respect of a young person by a justice who is not a youth court judge.

Interim release by youth court judge only

(8) Where a young person against whom proceedings have been taken under this Act is charged with an offence referred to in section 457.7 of the *Criminal Code*, a youth court judge, but no other court, judge or justice, may release the young person from custody under that section.

Review by court of appeal

(9) A decision made by a youth court judge under subsection (8) may be reviewed in accordance with section 608.1 of the *Criminal Code* and that section applies, with such modifications as the circumstances require, to any decision so made. 1986, c. 32, s. 6.

Notices to Parents

Notice to parent in case of arrest

9. (1) Subject to subsections (3) and (4), where a young person is arrested and detained in custody pending his appearance in court, the officer in charge at the time the young person is detained shall, as soon as possible, give or cause to be given, orally or in writing, to a parent of the young person notice of the arrest stating the place of detention and the reason for the arrest.

(2) Subject to subsections (3) and (4), where a summons or an appearance notice is issued in respect of a young person, the person who issued the summons or appearance notice, or, where a young person is released on giving his promise to appear or entering into a recognizance, the officer in charge, shall, as soon as possible, give or cause to be given, in writing, to a parent of the young person notice of the summons, appearance notice, promise to appear or recognizance. *Notice to parent in case of summons or appearance notice*

(3) Where the whereabouts of the parents of a young person *Notice to relative or other adult*
  (a) who is arrested and detained in custody,
  (b) in respect of whom a summons or an appearance notice is issued, or
  (c) who is released on giving his promise to appear or entering into a recognizance
are not known or it appears that no parent is available, a notice under this section may be given to an adult relative of the young person who is known to the young person and is likely to assist him or, if no such adult relative is available, to such other adult who is known to the young person and is likely to assist him as the person giving the notice considers appropriate.

(4) Where a young person described in paragraph (3)(a), (b) or (c) is married, a notice under this section may be given to the spouse of the young person instead of a parent. *Notice to spouse*

(5) Where doubt exists as to the person to whom a notice under this section should be given, a youth court judge or, where a youth court judge is, having regard to the circumstances, not reasonably available, a justice may give directions as to the person to whom the notice should be given, and a notice given in accordance with such directions is sufficient notice for the purposes of this section. *Notice on direction of youth court judge or justice*

(6) Any notice under this section shall, in addition to any other requirements under this section, include *Contents of notice*
  (a) the name of the young person in respect of whom it is given;
  (b) the charge against the young person and the time and place of appearance; and
  (c) a statement that the young person has the right to be represented by counsel.

(7) Subject to subsection (10), a notice under this section given in writing may be served personally or may be sent by mail. *Service of notice*

(8) Subject to subsection (9), failure to give notice in *Proceedings not invalid*

accordance with this section does not affect the validity of proceedings under this Act.

(9) Failure to give notice in accordance with subsection (2) in any case renders invalid any subsequent proceedings under this Act relating to the case unless

> (a) a parent of the young person against whom proceedings are held attends court with the young person; or
> (b) notice is given in accordance with paragraph (10)(a) or dispensed with pursuant to paragraph 10(b).

1986, c. 32, s. 7(1).

Where a notice not served

(10) Where there has been a failure to give a notice in accordance with this section and none of the persons to whom such notice may be given attends court with a young person, a youth court judge or a justice before whom proceedings are held against the young person may

> (a) adjourn the proceedings and order that the notice be given in such manner and to such person as he directs; or
> (b) dispense with the notice where, in his opinion, having regard to the circumstances, notice may be dispensed with.

Form of notices

(11) Repealed. 1986, c. 32, s. 7(2), effective September 1, 1986. 1986, c. 32, s. 7.

Order requiring attendance of parent

10. (1) Where a parent does not attend proceedings before a youth court in respect of a young person, the court may, if in its opinion the presence of the parent is necessary or in the best interest of the young person, by order in writing require the parent to attend at any stage of the proceedings.

Service of order

(2) A copy of any order made under subsection (1) shall be served by a peace officer or by a person designated by a youth court by delivering it personally to the parent to whom it is directed, unless the youth court authorizes service by registered mail. 1986, c. 32, s. 8(1).

Failure to attend

(3) A parent who is ordered to attend a youth court pursuant to subsection (1) and who fails without reasonable excuse, the proof of which lies on that parent, to comply with the order

> (a) is guilty of contempt of court;
> (b) may be dealt with summarily by the court; and
> (c) is liable to the punishment provided for in the *Criminal Code* for a summary conviction offence.

Appeal

(4) Section 9 of the *Criminal Code* applies where a person is convicted of contempt of court under subsection (3).

Warrant to arrest parent

(5) If a parent who is ordered to attend a youth court pursuant to subsection (1) does not attend at the time and

place named in the order or fails to remain in attendance as required and it is proved that a copy of the order was served on the parent, a youth court may issue a warrant to compel the attendance of the parent.

(6) Repealed. 1986, c. 32, s. 8 (2). 1986, c. 32, s. 8.

Form of warrant

Right to Counsel

11. (1) A young person has the right to retain and instruct counsel without delay, and to exercise that right personally, at any stage of proceedings against the young person and prior to and during any consideration of whether, instead of commencing or continuing judicial proceedings against the young person under this Act, to use alternative measures to deal with the young person. 1986, c. 32, s. 9.

Right to retain counsel

(2) Every young person who is arrested or detained shall, forthwith on his arrest or detention, be advised by the arresting officer or the officer in charge, as the case may be, of his right to be represented by counsel and shall be given an opportunity to obtain counsel.

Arresting officer to advise young person of right to counsel

(3) Where a young person is not represented by counsel
  (a) at a hearing at which it will be determined whether to release the young person or detain him in custody prior to disposition of his case,
  (b) at a hearing held pursuant to section 16,
  (c) at his trial, or
  (d) at a review of a disposition held before a youth court or a review board under this Act,
the justice before whom, or the youth court or review board before which, the hearing, trial or review is held shall advise the young person of his right to be represented by counsel and shall give the young person a reasonable opportunity to obtain counsel.

Justice, youth court or review board to advise young person of right to counsel

(4) Where a young person at his trial or at a hearing or review referred to in subsection (3) wishes to obtain counsel but is unable to do so, the youth court before which the hearing, trial or review is held or the review board before which the review is held
  (a) shall, where there is a legal aid or assistance program available in the province where the hearing, trial or review is held, refer the young person to that program for the appointment of counsel; or
  (b) where no legal aid or assistance program is available or the young person is unable to obtain counsel through such program, may, and on the request of the young person shall, direct that the young person be represented by counsel.

Trial, hearing or review before youth court or review board

(5) Where a direction is made under paragraph (4)(b) in respect of a young person, the Attorney General of the

Appointment of counsel

province in which the direction is made shall appoint counsel, or cause counsel to be appointed, to represent the young person.

Release hearing before justice

(6) Where a young person at a hearing before a justice who is not a youth court judge at which it will be determined whether to release the young person or detain him in custody prior to disposition of his case wishes to obtain counsel but is unable to do so, the justice shall
> (a) where there is a legal aid or assistance program available in the province where the hearing is held,
>> (i) refer the young person to that program for the appointment of counsel, or
>> (ii) refer the matter to a youth court to be dealt with in accordance with paragraph (4) (a) or (b); or
>
> (b) where no legal aid or assistance program is available or the young person is unable to obtain counsel through such program, refer the matter to a youth court to be dealt with in accordance with paragraph (4) (b).

Young person may be assisted by adult

(7) Where a young person is not represented by counsel at his trial or at a hearing or review referred to in subsection (3), the justice before whom or the youth court or review board before which the proceedings are held may, on the request of the young person, allow the young person to be assisted by an adult whom the justice, court or review board considers to be suitable.

Counsel independent of parents

(8) In any case where it appears to a youth court judge or a justice that the interests of a young person and his parents are in conflict or that it would be in the best interest of the young person to be represented by his own counsel, the judge or justice shall ensure that the young person is represented by counsel independent of his parents.

Statement of right to counsel

(9) A statement that a young person has the right to be represented by counsel shall be included in any appearance notice or summons issued to the young person, any warrant to arrest the young person, any promise to appear given by the young person, any recognizance entered into before an officer in charge by the young person or any notice of a review of a disposition given to the young person. 1986, c. 32, s. 9.

Appearance

Where young person appears

12. (1) Where a young person against whom an information is laid first appears before a youth court judge or a justice, the judge or justice shall
> (a) cause the information to be read to him; and
> (b) where the young person is not represented by counsel, inform him of his right to be so represented.

(2) A young person may waive the requirement under paragraph (1) (a) where the young person is represented by counsel.

Waiver

(3) Where a young person is not represented in youth court by counsel, the youth court shall, before accepting a plea,
  (a) satisfy itself that the young person understands the charge against him; and
  (b) explain to the young person that he may plead guilty or not guilty to the charge.

Where young person not represented by counsel

(4) Where the youth court is not satisfied that a young person understands the charge against him, as required under paragraph (3) (a), the court shall enter a plea of not guilty on behalf of the young person and shall proceed with the trial in accordance with subsection 19 (2).

Where youth court not satisfied

Medical and Psychological Reports

13. (1) For the purpose of
  (a) considering an application under section 16,
  (b) determining whether to direct that an issue be tried whether a young person is, on account of insanity, unfit to stand trial, or
  (c) making or reviewing a disposition under this Act,

a youth court may, at any stage of proceedings against a young person,

  (d) with the consent of the young person and the prosecutor, or
  (e) on its own motion or on the application of either the young person or the prosecutor, where the court has reasonable grounds to believe that the young person may be suffering from a physical or mental illness or disorder, a psychological disorder, an emotional disturbance, a learning disability or mental retardation and where the court believes a medical, psychological or psychiatric report in respect of the young person might be helpful in making any decision pursuant to this Act,

by order require that the young person be examined by a qualified person and that the person who conducts the examination report the results thereof in writing to the court.

Medical or psychological examination

(2) Where a youth court makes an order for an examination under subsection (1) for the purpose of determining whether to direct that an issue be tried whether a young person is, on account of insanity, unfit to stand trial, the examination shall be carried out by a qualified medical practitioner.

Examination for fitness to stand trial

(3) For the purpose of an examination under this section, a youth court may remand the young person who is to be examined to such custody as it directs for a period not

Custody for examination

exceeding eight days or, where it is satisfied that observation is required for a longer period to complete an examination or assessment and its opinion is supported by the evidence of, or a report in writing of, at least one qualified person, for a longer period not exceeding thirty days.

Disclosure of report

(4) Where a youth court receives a report made in respect of a young person pursuant to subsection (1),
    (a) the court shall, subject to subsection (6), cause a copy of the report to be given to
        (i) the young person,
        (ii) a parent of the young person, if the parent is in attendance at the proceedings against the young person,
        (iii) counsel, if any, representing the young person, and
        (iv) the prosecutor; and
    (b) the court may cause a copy of the report to be given to a parent of the young person not in attendance at the proceedings against the young person if the parent is, in the opinion of the court, taking an active interest in the proceedings.

Cross-examination

(5) Where a report is made in respect of a young person pursuant to subsection (1), the young person, his counsel or the adult assisting him pursuant to subsection 11(7) and the prosecutor shall, subject to subsection (6), on application to the youth court, be given an opportunity to cross-examine the person who made the report.

Report may be withheld from young person, parents or prosecutor

(6) A youth court may withhold the whole or any part of a report made in respect of a young person pursuant to subsection (1) from
    (a) a private prosecutor where disclosure of the report or part thereof, in the opinion of the court, is not necessary for the prosecution of the case and might be prejudicial to the young person; or
    (b) the young person, his parents or a private prosecutor where the person who made the report states in writing that disclosure of the report or part thereof would be likely to be detrimental to the treatment or recovery of the young person or would be likely to result in bodily harm to, or be detrimental to the mental condition of, a third party.

Insanity at time of proceedings

(7) A youth court may, at any time before an adjudication in respect of a young person charged with an offence, where it appears that there is sufficient reason to doubt that the young person is, on account of insanity, capable of conducting his defence, direct that an issue be tried as to whether the young person is then on account of insanity unfit to stand trial.

(8) Where a youth court directs the trial of an issue under subsection (7), it shall proceed in accordance with section 543 of the *Criminal Code* in so far as that section may be applied. — Section 543 of Criminal Code to apply

(9) A report made pursuant to subsection (1) shall form part of the record of the case in respect of which it was requested. — Report to be part of record

(10) Notwithstanding any other provision of this Act, a qualified person who is of the opinion that a young person held in detention or committed to custody is likely to endanger his own life or safety or to endanger the life of, or cause bodily harm to, another person may immediately so advise any person who has the care and custody of the young person whether or not the same information is contained in a report made pursuant to subsection (1). — Disclosure by qualified person

(11) In this section, "qualified person" means a person duly qualified by provincial law to practice medicine or psychiatry or to carry out psychological examinations or assessments, as the circumstances require, or, where no such law exists, a person who is, in the opinion of the youth court, so qualified, and includes a person or a person within a class of persons designated by the Lieutenant Governor in Council of a province or his delegate. — Definition of "qualified person"

(12) Repealed. 1986, c. 32, s. 10, effective September 1, 1986. 1986, c. 32, s. 10. — Form of order

Pre-Disposition Report

14. (1) Where a youth court deems it advisable before making a disposition under section 20 in respect of a young person who is found guilty of an offence it may, and where a youth court is required under this Act to consider a pre-disposition report before making an order or a disposition in respect of a young person it shall, require the provincial director to cause to be prepared a pre-disposition report in respect of the young person and to submit the report to the court. — Pre-disposition report

(2) A pre-disposition report made in respect of a young person shall, subject to subsection (3), be in writing and shall include — Contents of report
- (a) the results of an interview with the young person and, where reasonably possible, the results of an interview with the parents of the young person;
- (b) the results of an interview with the victim in the case, where applicable and where reasonably possible; and
- (c) such information as is applicable to the case including, where applicable,
    - (i) the age, maturity, character, behaviour and attitude of the young person and his willingness to make amends,

(ii) any plans put forward by the young person to change his conduct or to participate in activities or undertake measures to improve himself,

(iii) the history of previous findings of delinquency under the *Juvenile Delinquents Act* or previous findings of guilt under this or any other Act of Parliament or any regulation made thereunder or under an Act of the legislature of a province or any regulation made thereunder or a by-law or ordinance of a municipality, the history of community or other services rendered to the young person with respect to such findings and the response of the young person to previous sentences or dispositions and to services rendered to him,

(iv) the history of alternative measures used to deal with the young person and the response of the young person thereto,

(v) the availability of community services and facilities for young persons and the willingness of the young person to avail himself of such services or facilities,

(vi) the relationship between the young person and his parents and the degree of control and influence of the parents over the young person, and

(vii) the school attendance and performance record and the employment record of the young person.

1986, c. 32, s. 11.

Oral report with leave

(3) Where a predisposition report cannot reasonably be committed to writing, it may, with leave of the youth court, be submitted orally in court.

Report to form part of record

(4) A pre-disposition report shall form part of the record of the case in respect of which it was requested.

Copies of pre-disposition report

(5) Where a pre-disposition report made in respect of a young person is submitted to a youth court in writing, the court

(a) shall, subject to subsection (7), cause a copy of the report to be given to

(i) the young person,

(ii) a parent of the young person, if the parent is in attendance at the proceedings against the young person,

(iii) counsel, if any, representing the young person, and

(iv) the prosecutor; and

(b) may cause a copy of the report to be given to a parent of the young person not in attendance at the proceedings against the young person if the parent is, in the opinion of the court, taking an active interest in the proceedings.

(6) Where a pre-disposition report made in respect of a young person is submitted to a youth court, the young person, his counsel or the adult assisting him pursuant to subsection 11(7) and the prosecutor shall, subject to subsection (7), on application to the youth court, be given the opportunity to cross-examine the person who made the report. Cross-examination

(7) Where a pre-disposition report made in respect of a young person is submitted to a youth court, the court may, where the prosecutor is a private prosecutor and disclosure of the report or any part thereof to the prosecutor might, in the opinion of the court, be prejudicial to the young person and is not, in the opinion of the court, necessary for the prosecution of the case against the young person, Report may be withheld from young person or private prosecutor

    (a) withhold the report or part thereof from the prosecutor, if the report is submitted in writing; or

    (b) exclude the prosecutor from the court during the submission of the report or part thereof, if the report is submitted orally in court.

(8) Where a pre-disposition report made in respect of a young person is submitted to a youth court, the court Report disclosed to other persons

    (a) shall, on request, cause a copy or a transcript of the report to be supplied to

        (i) any court that is dealing with matters relating to the young person, and

        (ii) any youth worker to whom the young person's case has been assigned; and

    (b) may, on request, cause a copy or a transcript of the report, or a part thereof, to be supplied to any person not otherwise authorized under this section to receive a copy or transcript of the report if, in the opinion of the court, the person has a valid interest in the proceedings.

(9) A provincial director who submits a pre-disposition report made in respect of a young person to a youth court may make the report, or any part thereof, available to any person in whose custody or under whose supervision the young person is placed or to any other person who is directly assisting in the care or treatment of the young person. Disclosure by the provincial director

(10) No statement made by a young person in the course of the preparation of a pre-disposition report in respect of the young person is admissible in evidence against him in any civil or criminal proceedings except in proceedings under section 16 or 20 or sections 28 to 32. Inadmissibility of statements

Disqualification of judge

15. (1) Subject to subsection (2), a youth court judge who, prior to an adjudication in respect of a young person charged with an offence, examines a pre-disposition report made in respect of the young person, or hears an application under section 16 in respect of the young person, in connection with that offence shall not in any capacity conduct or continue the trial of the young person for the offence and shall transfer the case to another judge to be dealt with according to law.

Exception

(2) A youth court judge may, in the circumstances referred to in subsection (1), with the consent of the young person and the prosecutor, conduct or continue the trial of the young person if the judge is satisfied that he has not been predisposed by information contained in the pre-disposition report or by representations made in respect of the application under section 16.

Transfer to Ordinary Court

Transfer to ordinary court

16. (1) At any time after an information is laid against a young person alleged to have, after attaining the age of fourteen years, committed an indictable offence other than an offence referred to in section 483 of the *Criminal Code* but prior to adjudication, a youth court may, on application of the young person or his counsel, or the Attorney General or his agent, after affording both parties and the parents of the young person an opportunity to be heard, if the court is of the opinion that, in the interest of society and having regard to the needs of the young person, the young person should be proceeded against in ordinary court, order that the young person be so proceeded against in accordance with the law ordinarily applicable to an adult charged with the offence.

Considerations by youth court

(2) In considering an application under subsection (1) in respect of a young person, a youth court shall take into account

(a) the seriousness of the alleged offence and the circumstances in which it was allegedly committed;

(b) the age, maturity, character and background of the young person and any record or summary of previous findings of delinquency under the *Juvenile Delinquents Act* or previous findings of guilt under this or any other Act of Parliament or any regulation made thereunder;

(c) the adequacy of this Act, and the adequacy of the *Criminal Code* or other Act of Parliament that would apply in respect of the young person if an order were made under subsection (1), to meet the circumstances of the case;

(d) the availability of treatment or correctional resources;

(e) any representations made to the court by or on behalf of the young person or by the Attorney General or his agent; and

(f) any other factors that the court considers relevant.

(3) In considering an application under subsection (1), a youth court shall consider a pre-disposition report.

(4) Notwithstanding subsections (1) and (3), where an application is made under subsection (1) by the Attorney General or his agent in respect of an offence alleged to have been committed by a young person while the young person was being proceeded against in ordinary court pursuant to an order previously made under that subsection or serving a sentence as a result of proceedings in ordinary court, the youth court may make a further order under that subsection without a hearing and without considering a pre-disposition report.

(5) Where a youth court makes an order or refuses to make an order under subsection (1), it shall state the reasons for its decision and the reasons shall form part of the record of the proceedings in the youth court.

(6) Where a youth court refuses to make an order under subsection (1) in respect of an alleged offence, no further application may be made under this section in respect of that offence.

(7) Where an order is made under subsection (1), proceedings under this Act shall be discontinued and the young person against whom the proceedings are taken shall be taken before the ordinary court.

(8) Where an order is made under subsection (1) that a young person be proceeded against in ordinary court in respect of an offence, that court has jurisdiction only in respect of that offence or an offence included therein.

(9) Subject to subsection (11), an order made in respect of a young person under subsection (1) or a refusal to make such an order shall, on application of the young person or his counsel or the Attorney General or his agent made within thirty days after the decision of the youth court, be reviewed by the superior court and that court may, in its discretion, confirm or reverse the decision of the youth court.

(10) A decision made in respect of a young person by a superior court under subsection (9) may, on application of the young person or his counsel or the Attorney General or his agent made within thirty days after the decision of the superior court, with the leave of the court of appeal, be reviewed by that court, and the court of appeal may, in its discretion, confirm or reverse the decision of the superior court.

(11) In any province where the youth court is a superior court, a review under subsection (9) shall be made by the court of appeal of the province.

Pre-disposition reports

Where young person on transfer status

Court to state reasons

No further applications for transfer

Effect of order under subsection (1)

Jurisdiction of ordinary court limited

Review of youth court decision

Review of superior court decision

Where the youth court is a superior court

Extension of time to make application

(12) A court to which an application is made under subsection (9) or (10) may at any time extend the time within which the application may be made.

Notice of application

(13) A person who proposes to apply for a review under subsection (9) or (10) or for leave to apply for a review under subsection (10) shall give notice of his application for a review or for leave to apply for a review in such manner and within such period of time as may be directed by rules of court.

Form of transfer to ordinary court

(14) Repealed. 1986, c. 32, s. 12, effective September 1, 1986. 1986, c. 32, s. 12.

Order restricting publication of information presented at transfer hearing

17. (1) Where a youth court hears an application for a transfer to ordinary court under section 16, it shall
   (a) where the young person is not represented by counsel, or
   (b) on application made by or on behalf of the young person or the prosecutor, where the young person is represented by counsel,
make an order directing that any information respecting the offence presented at the hearing shall not be published in any newspaper or broadcast before such time as
   (c) an order for a transfer is refused or set aside on review and the time for all reviews against the decision has expired or all proceedings in respect of any such review have been completed; or
   (d) the trial is ended, if the case is transferred to ordinary court.

Offence

(2) Every one who fails to comply with an order made pursuant to subsection (1) is guilty of an offence punishable on summary conviction.

Meaning of "newspaper"

(3) In this section, "newspaper" has the meaning set out in section 261 of the *Criminal Code*.

Transfer of Jurisdiction

Transfer of jurisdiction

18. (1) Notwithstanding subsections 434(1) and (3) of the *Criminal Code*, where a young person is charged with an offence that is alleged to have been committed in one province, he may, if the Attorney General of the province where the offence is alleged to have been committed consents, appear before a youth court of any other province and,
   (a) where the young person signifies his consent to plead guilty and pleads guilty to that offence, the court shall, if it is satisfied that the facts support the charge, find the young person guilty of the offence alleged in the information; and
   (b) where the young person does not signify his consent to plead guilty and does not plead guilty, or where the court is not satisfied that the facts

support the charge, the young person shall, if he was detained in custody prior to his appearance, be returned to custody and dealt with according to law.

(2) Where a person is charged with an offence that is alleged to have been committed in a province in which he is a young person, that person may be proceeded against in accordance with subsection 434(3) of the *Criminal Code* before the ordinary court in another province in which he is an adult. Young person transferred to ordinary court in other province

(3) Where a person is charged with an offence that is alleged to have been committed in a province in which he is an adult, he may be proceeded with in accordance with subsection (1) before a youth court in another province in which he is a young person. Adult transferred to youth court in other province

Adjudication

19. (1) Where a young person pleads guilty to an offence charged against him and the youth court is satisfied that the facts support the charge, the court shall find the young person guilty of the offence. Where young person pleads guilty

(2) Where a young person pleads not guilty to an offence charged against him, or where a young person pleads guilty but the youth court is not satisfied that the facts support the charge, the court shall proceed with the trial and shall, after considering the matter, find the young person guilty or not guilty or make an order dismissing the charge, as the case may be. Where young person pleads not guilty

(3) The court shall not make a finding under this section in respect of a young person in respect of whom an application may be made under section 16 for an order that the young person be proceeded against in ordinary court unless it has inquired as to whether any of the parties to the proceedings wishes to make such an application, and, if any party so wishes, has given that party an opportunity to do so. 1986, c. 32, s. 13. 1986, c. 32, s. 13. Application for transfer to ordinary court

Dispositions

20. (1) Where a youth court finds a young person guilty of an offence, it shall consider any pre-disposition report required by the court, any representations made by the parties to the proceedings or their counsel or agents and by the parents of the young person and any other relevant information before the court, and the court shall then make any one of the following dispositions, or any number thereof that are not inconsistent with each other: Dispositions that may be made

(a) by order direct that the young person be discharged absolutely, if the court considers it to be in the best interests of the young person and not contrary to the public interest;

(b) impose on the young person a fine not exceeding one thousand dollars to be paid at such time and on such terms as the court may fix;

(c) order the young person to pay to any other person at such time and on such terms as the court may fix an amount by way of compensation for loss of or damage to property, for loss of income or support or for special damages for personal injury arising from the commission of the offence where the value thereof is readily ascertainable, but no order shall be made for general damages;

(d) order the young person to make restitution to any other person of any property obtained by the young person as a result of the commission of the offence within such time as the court may fix, if the property is owned by that other person or was, at the time of the offence, in his lawful possession;

(e) if any property obtained as a result of the commission of the offence has been sold to an innocent purchaser, where restitution of the property to its owner or any other person has been made or ordered, order the young person to pay the purchaser, at such time and on such terms as the court may fix, an amount not exceeding the amount paid by the purchaser for the property;

(f) subject to section 21, order the young person to compensate any person in kind or by way of personal services at such time and on such terms as the court may fix for any loss, damage or injury suffered by that person in respect of which an order may be made under paragraph (c) or (e);

(g) subject to section 21, order the young person to perform a community service at such time and on such terms as the court may fix;

(h) make any order of prohibition, seizure or forfeiture that may be imposed under any Act of Parliament or any regulation made thereunder where an accused is found guilty or convicted of that offence;

(i) subject to section 22, by order direct that the young person be detained for treatment, subject to such conditions as the court considers appropriate, in a hospital or other place where treatment is available, where a report has been made in respect of the young person pursuant to subsection 13(1) that recommends that the young person undergo treatment for a condition referred in paragraph 13(1)(e);

(j) place the young person on probation in accordance with section 23 for a specified period not exceeding two years;

(k) subject to section 24, commit the young person to custody, to be served continuously or intermittently, for a specified period not exceeding
    (i) two years from the date of committal, or
    (ii) where the young person is found guilty of an offence for which the punishment provided by the *Criminal Code* or any other Act of Parliament is imprisonment for life, three years from the date of committal; and
(l) impose on the young person such other reasonable and ancillary conditions as it deems advisable and in the best interest of the young person and the public.

(2) A disposition made under this section shall come into force on the date on which it is made or on such later date as the youth court specifies therein.   *Coming into force of disposition*

(3) No disposition made under this section, except an order made under paragraph (1)(h) or (k), shall continue in force for more than two years and, where the youth court makes more than one disposition at the same time in respect of the same offence, the combined duration of the dispositions, except in respect of an order made under paragraph (1)(h) or (k), shall not exceed two years.   *Duration of disposition*

(4) Subject to subsection (4.1), where more than one disposition is made under this section in respect of a young person with respect to different offences, the continuous combined duration of those dispositions shall not exceed three years. 1986, c. 32, s. 14(1).   *Combined duration of dispositions*

(4.1) Where a disposition is made under this section in respect of an offence committed by a young person after the commencement of, but before the completion of, any dispositions made in respect of previous offences committed by the young person,   *Duration of dispositions made at different times*
  (a) the duration of the disposition made in respect of the subsequent offence shall be determined in accordance with subsections (3) and (4);
  (b) the disposition may be served consecutively to the dispositions made in respect of the previous offences; and
  (c) the combined duration of all the dispositions may exceed three years.
1986, c. 32, s. 14(1).

(5) Subject to section 668 of the *Criminal Code*, a disposition made under this section shall continue in effect in accordance with the terms thereof, after the young person against whom it is made becomes an adult. 1986, c. 32, s. 14(1).   *Disposition continues when adult*

(6) Where a youth court makes a disposition under this section, it shall state its reasons therefor in the record of the case and shall   *Reasons for the disposition*

(a) provide or cause to be provided a copy of the disposition, and

(b) on request, provide or cause to be provided a transcript or copy of the reasons for the disposition to the young person in respect of whom the disposition was made, his counsel, his parents, the provincial director, where the provincial director has an interest in the disposition, the prosecutor and, in the case of a custodial disposition made under paragraph (1)(k), the review board, if any has been established or designated.

Limitation on punishment

(7) No disposition shall be made in respect of a young person under this section that results in a punishment that is greater than the maximum punishment that would be applicable to an adult who has committed the same offence.

Application of Part XX of Criminal Code

(8) Part XX of the *Criminal Code* does not apply in respect of proceedings under this Act except for sections 683, 685 and 686 and subsections 655(2) to (5) and 662.1(2), which provisions apply with such modifications as the circumstances require.

Section 722 of Criminal Code does not apply

(9) Section 722 of the *Criminal Code* does not apply in respect of proceedings under this Act.

Contents of probation order

(10) The youth court shall specify in any probation order made under paragraph (1)(j) the period for which it is to remain in force. 1986, c. 32, s. 14(2). 1986, c. 32, s. 14.

Where a fine or other payment is ordered

21. (1) The youth court shall, in imposing a fine on a young person under paragraph 20(1)(b) or in making an order against a young person under paragraph 20(1)(c) or (e), have regard to the present and future means of the young person to pay.

Fine option program

(2) A young person against whom a fine is imposed under paragraph 20(1)(b) may discharge the fine in whole or in part by earning credits for work performed in a program established for that purpose

(a) by the Lieutenant Governor in Council of the province in which the fine was imposed; or

(b) by the Lieutenant Governor in Council of the province in which the young person resides, where an appropriate agreement is in effect between the government of that province and the government of the province in which the fine was imposed.

Rates, crediting and other matters

(3) A program referred to in subsection (2) shall determine the rate at which credits are earned and may provide for the manner of crediting any amounts earned against the fine and any other matters necessary for or incidental to carrying out the program.

Representations respecting orders under paras. 20(1)(c) to (f)

(4) In considering whether to make an order under paragraphs 20(1)(c) and (f), the youth court may con-

sider any representations made by the person who would be compensated or to whom restitution or payment would be made.

(5) Where the youth court makes an order under paragraphs 20(1)(c) to (f), it shall cause notice of the terms of the order to be given to the person who is to be compensated or to whom restitution or payment is to be made.
Notice of orders under paras. 20(1)(c) to (f)

(6) No order may be made under paragraph 20(1)(f) unless the youth court has secured the consent of the person to be compensated.
Consent of person to be compensated

(7) No order may be made under paragraph 20(1)(f) or (g) unless the youth court
(a) is satisfied that the young person against whom the order is made is a suitable candidate for such an order; and
(b) is satisfied that the order does not interfere with the normal hours of work or education of the young person.
Order for compensation or community service

(8) No order may be made under paragraph 20(1)(f) or (g) to perform personal or community services unless such services can be completed in two hundred and forty hours or less and within twelve months of the date of the order.
Duration of order for service

(9) No order may be made under paragraph 20(1)(g) unless
(a) the community service to be performed is part of a program that is approved by the provincial director; or
(b) the youth court is satisfied that the person or organization for whom the community service is to be performed has agreed to its performance.
1986, c. 32, s. 15.
Community service order

(10) A youth court may, on application by or on behalf of the young person in respect of whom a disposition has been made under paragraphs 20(1)(b) to (g), allow further time for the completion of the disposition subject to any regulations made pursuant to paragraph 67(b) and to any rules made by the youth court pursuant to subsection 68(1). 1986, c. 32, s. 15.
Application for further time to complete disposition

22. (1) No order may be made under paragraph 20(1)(i) unless the youth court has secured the consent of the young person, the parents of the young person and the hospital or other place where the young person is to be detained for treatment.
Consent for treatment order

(2) The youth court may dispense with the consent of a parent required under subsection (1) if it appears that the parent is not available or if the parent is not, in the opinion of the court, taking an active interest in the proceedings.
Where consent of parent dispensed with

Conditions that must appear in probation orders

23. (1) The following conditions shall be included in a probation order made under paragraph 20(1)(j):
  (a) that the young person bound by the probation order shall keep the peace and be of good behaviour; and
  (b) that the young person appear before the youth court when required by the court to do so.
1986, c. 32, s. 16 (1).

Conditions that may appear in probation orders

(2) A probation order made under paragraph 20(1)(j) may include such of the following conditions as the youth court considers appropriate in the circumstances of the case:
  (a) that the young person bound by the probation order report to and be under the supervision of the provincial director or a person designated by the youth court;
  (a.1) that the young person notify the clerk of the youth court, the provincial director or the youth worker assigned to his case of any change of address or any change in his place of employment, education or training;
  (b) that the young person remain within the territorial jurisdiction of one or more courts named in the order;
  (c) that the young person make reasonable efforts to obtain and maintain suitable employment;
  (d) that the young person attend school or such other place of learning, training or recreation as is appropriate, if the court is satisfied that a suitable program is available for the young person at such place;
  (e) that the young person reside with a parent, or such other adult as the court considers appropriate, who is willing to provide for the care and maintenance of the young person;
  (f) that the young person reside in such place as the provincial director may specify; and
  (g) that the young person comply with such other reasonable conditions set out in the order as the court considers desirable, including conditions for securing the good conduct of the young person and for preventing the commission by the young person of other offences.
1986, c. 32, ss. 16(2), (3).

Communication of probation order to young person and parent

(3) Where the youth court makes a probation order under paragraph 20(1)(j), it shall
  (a) cause the order to be read by or to the young person bound by the probation order;
  (b) explain or cause to be explained to the young person the purpose and effect of the order and

ascertain that the young person understands it; and

(c) cause a copy of the order to be given to the young person and to a parent of the young person, if the parent is in attendance at the proceedings against the young person.

(4) Where the youth court makes a probation order under paragraph 20(1)(j), it may cause a copy of the report to be given to a parent of the young person not in attendance at the proceedings against the young person if the parent is, in the opinion of the court, taking an active interest in the proceedings. *Copy of probation order to parent*

(5) After a probation order has been read by or to a young person and explained to him pursuant to subsection (3), the young person shall endorse the order acknowledging that he has received a copy of the order and acknowledging the fact that it has been explained to him. *Endorsement of order by young person*

(6) The failure of a young person to endorse a probation order pursuant to subsection (5) does not affect the validity of the order. *Validity of probation order*

(7) A probation order made under paragraph 20(1)(j) comes into force *Commencement of probation order*
    (a) on the date on which the order is made; or
    (b) where the young person in respect of whom the order is made is committed to continuous custody, on the expiration of the period of custody.

(8) A young person may be given notice to appear before the youth court pursuant to paragraph (1)(b) orally or in writing, and where the notice is in writing it may be in Form 9. *Notice to appear*

(9) If a young person to whom a notice is given in writing to appear before the youth court pursuant to paragraph (1)(b) does not appear at the time and place named in the notice and it is proved that a copy of the notice was served on him, a youth court may issue a warrant to compel the appearance of the young person. 1986, c. 32, s. 16. *Warrant to arrest young person*

24. (1) The youth court shall not commit a young person to custody under paragraph 20(1)(k) unless the court considers a committal to custody to be necessary for the protection of society having regard to the seriousness of the offence and the circumstances in which it was committed and having regard to the needs and circumstances of the young person. *Conditions for custody*

(2) Subject to subsection (3), before making an order of committal to custody, the youth court shall consider a pre-disposition report. *Pre-disposition report*

(3) The youth court may, with the consent of the prosecutor and the young person or his counsel, dispense with *Report dispensed with*

the pre-disposition report required under subsection (2) if the youth court is satisfied, having regard to the circumstances, that the report is unnecessary or that it would not be in the best interests of the young person to require one. 1986, c. 32, s. 17.

Definitions

"open custody"

24.1 (1) In this section and sections 24.2, 24.3, 28 and 29, "open custody" means custody in
- (a) a community residential centre, group home, child care institution, or forest or wilderness camp, or
- (b) any other like place or facility designated by the Lieutenant Governor in Council of a province or his delegate as a place of open custody for the purposes of this Act, and includes a place or facility within a class of such places or facilities so designated;

"secure custody"

"secure custody" means custody in a place or facility designated by the Lieutenant Governor in Council of a province for the secure containment or restraint of young persons, and includes a place or facility within a class of such places or facilities so designated.

Order of committal to specify type of custody

(2) Where the youth court commits a young person to custody under paragraph 20(1)(k), it shall specify in the order of committal whether the custody is to be open custody or secure custody.

Conditions for secure custody

(3) Subject to subsection (4), no young person who is found guilty of an offence shall be committed to secure custody unless the young person was, at the time the offence was committed, fourteen years of age or more and unless
- (a) the offence is one for which an adult would be liable to imprisonment for five years or more;
- (b) the offence is an offence under section 26 of this Act in relation to a disposition under paragraph 20(1)(j), an offence under section 132 (prison breach) or subsection 133(1) (escape or being at large without excuse) of the *Criminal Code* or an attempt to commit any such offence; or
- (c) the offence is an indictable offence and the young person was
  - (i) within twelve months prior to the commission of the offence, found guilty of an offence for which an adult would be liable to imprisonment for five years or more, or adjudged to have committed a delinquency under the *Juvenile Delinquents Act* in respect of such offence, or
  - (ii) at any time prior to the commission of the offence, committed to secure custody with respect to a previous offence, or committed to custody in a place or facility for the secure

containment or restraint of a child, within the meaning of the *Juvenile Delinquents Act,* with respect to a delinquency under that Act.

(4) A young person who is found guilty of an offence and who was, at the time the offence was committed, under the age of fourteen years may be committed to secure custody if   *Idem*
- (a) the offence is one for which an adult would be liable to life imprisonment;
- (b) the offence is one for which an adult would be liable to imprisonment for five years or more and the young person was at any time prior to the commission of the offence found guilty of an offence for which an adult would be liable to imprisonment for five years or more or adjudged to have committed a delinquency under the *Juvenile Delinquents Act* in respect of such offence; or
- (c) the offence is an offence under section 26 of this Act in relation to a disposition under paragraph 20(1)(j), an offence under section 132 (prison breach) or subsection 133(1) (escape or being at large without excuse) of the *Criminal Code* or an attempt to commit any such offence.

1986, c. 32, s. 17.

24.2 (1) Subject to this section and sections 24.3 and 24.5, a young person who is committed to custody shall be placed in open custody or secure custody, as specified in the order of committal, at such place or facility as the provincial director may specify.   Place of custody

(2) Where a young person is committed to custody, the youth court shall issue or cause to be issued a warrant of committal.   Warrant of committal

(3) A young person who is committed to custody may, in the course of being transferred from custody to the court or from the court to custody, be held under the supervision and control of a peace officer or in such place of temporary detention referred to in subsection 7(1) as the provincial director may specify.   Exception

(4) Subject to this section and section 24.5, a young person who is committed to custody shall be held separate and apart from any adult who is detained or held in custody.   Young person to be held separate from adults

(5) Subsection 7(2) applies, with such modifications as the circumstances require, in respect of a person held in a place of temporary detention pursuant to subsection (3).   Subsection 7(2) applies

(6) A young person who is committed to custody may, during the period of custody, be transferred by the provincial director from one place or facility of open   Transfer

custody to another or from one place or facility of secure custody to another.

Transfer from secure to open custody

(7) No young person who is committed to secure custody may be transferred to a place or facility of open custody except in accordance with sections 28 to 31.

No transfer from open custody to secure custody

(8) Subject to subsection (9), no young person who is committed to open custody may be transferred to a place or facility of secure custody.

Exception

(9) The provincial director may transfer a young person from a place or facility of open custody to a place or facility of secure custody for a period not exceeding fifteen days if

(a) the young person escapes or attempts to escape lawful custody; or

(b) the transfer is, in the opinion of the provincial director, necessary for the safety of the young person or the safety of others in the place or facility of open custody.

1986, c. 32, s. 17.

Consecutive dispositions of custody

24.3. (1) Where a young person is committed to open custody and secure custody, any portions of which dispositions are to be served consecutively, the disposition of secure custody shall be served first without regard to the order in which the dispositions were imposed.

Concurrent dispositions of custody

(2) Where a young person is committed to open custody and secure custody, any portions of which dispositions are to be served concurrently, the concurrent portions of the dispositions shall be served in secure custody.

1986, c. 32, s. 17.

Committal to custody deemed continuous

24.4 (1) A young person who is committed to custody under paragraph 20(1)(k) shall be deemed to be committed to continuous custody unless the youth court specifies otherwise.

Availability of place of intermittent custody

(2) Before making an order of committal to intermittent custody under paragraph 20(1)(k), the youth court shall require the prosecutor to make available to the court for its consideration a report of the provincial director as to the availability of a place of custody in which an order of intermittent custody can be enforced and, where the report discloses that no such place of custody is available, the court shall not make the order. 1986, c. 32, s. 17.

Transfer to adult facility

24.5. (1) Where a young person is committed to custody under paragraph 20(1)(k), the youth court may, on application of the provincial director made at any time after the young person attains the age of eighteen years, after affording the young person an opportunity to be heard, authorize the provincial director to direct that the young person serve his disposition or the remaining portion thereof in a provincial correctional facility for adults, if the court considers it to be in the best interests of the young person or in the public interest, but in that event, the provisions of this Act shall continue to apply in respect of that person.

(2) Where a young person is committed to custody under paragraph 20(1)(k) and is concurrently under sentence of imprisonment imposed in ordinary court, that person may, in the discretion of the provincial director, serve his disposition and sentence, or any portion thereof, in a place of custody for young persons, in a provincial correctional facility for adults, or where the unexpired portion of the sentence is two years or more, in a penitentiary. 1986, c. 32, s. 17.

Where disposition and sentence concurrent

25. (1) Where a disposition has been made under paragraphs 20(1)(b) to (g) or paragraph 20(1)(i), (j) or (l) in respect of a young person and the young person or a parent with whom he resides is or becomes a resident of a territorial division outside the jurisdiction of the youth court that made the disposition, whether in the same or in another province, a youth court judge in the territorial division in which the disposition was made may, on the application of the Attorney General or his agent or on the application of the young person or his parent with the consent of the Attorney General or his agent, transfer the disposition and such portion of the record of the case as is appropriate to a youth court in the other territorial division, and all subsequent proceedings relating to the case shall thereafter be carried out and enforced by that court. 1986, c. 32, s. 18.

Transfer of disposition

(2) No disposition may be transferred from one province to another under this section until the time for an appeal against the disposition or the finding on which the disposition was based has expired or until all proceedings in respect of any such appeal have been completed.

No transfer outside province before appeal completed

(3) Where an application is made under subsection (1) to transfer the disposition of a young person to a province in which the young person is an adult, a youth court judge may, with the consent of the Attorney General, transfer the disposition and the record of the case to the youth court in the province to which the transfer is sought, and the youth court to which the case is transferred shall have full jurisdiction in respect of the disposition as if that court had made the disposition, and the person shall be further dealt with in accordance with this Act. 1986, c. 32, s. 18.

Transfer to a province where person is adult

25.1 (1) Where a disposition has been made under paragraphs 20(1)(i) to (k) in respect of a young person, the disposition in one province may be dealt with in any other province pursuant to any agreement that may have been made between the two provinces.

Interprovincial arrangements for treatment, probation or custody

(2) Subject to subsection (3), where a disposition made

Youth court retains jurisdiction

in respect of a young person is dealt with pursuant to this section in a province other than that in which the disposition was made, the youth court of the province in which the disposition was made shall, for all purposes of this Act, retain exclusive jurisdiction over the young person as if the disposition were dealt with within that province, and any warrant or process issued in respect of the young person may be executed or served in any place in Canada outside the province where the disposition was made as if it were executed or served in that province.

Waiver of jurisdiction

(3) Where a disposition made in respect of a young person is dealt with pursuant to this section in a province other than that in which the disposition was made, the youth court of the province in which the disposition was made may, with the consent in writing of the Attorney General of that province or his delegate and the young person, waive its jurisdiction, for the purpose of any proceeding under this Act, to the youth court of the province in which the disposition is dealt with, in which case the youth court in the province in which the disposition is so dealt with shall have full jurisdiction in respect of the disposition as if that court had made the disposition. 1986, c. 32, s. 19.

Failure to comply with disposition

26. A person who is subject to a disposition made under paragraphs 20(1)(b) to (g) or paragraph 20(1)(j) or (l) and who wilfully fails or refuses to comply with that order is guilty of an offence punishable on summary conviction. 1986, c. 32, s. 19.

Appeals

Appeals for indictable offences

27. (1) An appeal lies under this Act in respect of an indictable offence or an offence that the Attorney General or his agent elects to proceed with as an indictable offence in accordance with Part XVIII of the *Criminal Code*, which Part applies with such modifications as the circumstances require. 1986, c. 32, s. 20(1).

Appeals for summary conviction offences

(1.1) An appeal lies under this Act in respect of an offence punishable on summary conviction or an offence that the Attorney General or his agent elects to proceed with as an offence punishable on summary conviction in accordance with Part XXIV of the *Criminal Code*, which Part applies with such modifications as the circumstances require. 1986, c. 32, s. 20(1).

Deemed election

(2) For the purpose of appeal under this Act, where no election is made in respect of an offence that may be prosecuted by indictment or proceeded with by way of summary conviction, the Attorney General or his agent shall be deemed to have elected to proceed with the offence as an offence punishable on summary conviction.

(3) In any province where the youth court is a superior court, an appeal under subsection (1.1) shall be made to the court of appeal of the province. 1986, c. 32, s. 20(2). *Where the youth court is a superior court*

(4) In any province where the youth court is a county or district court, an appeal under subsection (1.1) shall be made to the superior court of the province. 1986, c. 32, s. 20(2). *Where the youth court is a county or district court*

(5) No appeal lies pursuant to subsection (1) from a judgment of the court of appeal in respect of a finding of guilt or an order dismissing an information to the Supreme Court of Canada unless leave to appeal is granted by the Supreme Court of Canada within twenty-one days after the judgment of the court of appeal is pronounced or within such extended time as the Supreme Court of Canada or a judge thereof may, for special reasons, allow. 1986, c. 32, s. 20(2). *Appeal to the Supreme Court of Canada*

(6) No appeal lies from a disposition under sections 28 to 32. 1986, c. 32, s. 20. *No appeal from disposition on review*

Review of Dispositions

28. (1) Where a young person is committed to custody pursuant to a disposition made in respect of an offence for a period exceeding one year, the provincial director of the province in which the young person is held in custody shall cause the young person to be brought before the youth court forthwith at the end of one year from the date of the most recent disposition made in respect of the offence, and the youth court shall review the disposition. *Automatic review of disposition involving custody*

(2) Where a young person is committed to custody pursuant to dispositions made in respect of more than one offence for a total period exceeding one year, the provincial director of the province in which the young person is held in custody shall cause the young person to be brought before the youth court forthwith at the end of one year from the date of the earliest disposition made, and the youth court shall review the dispositions. *Idem*

(3) Where a young person is committed to custody pursuant to a disposition made in respect of an offence, the provincial director may, on his own initiative, and shall, on the request of the young person, his parent or the Attorney General or his agent, on any of the grounds set out in subsection (4), cause the young person to be brought before the youth court at any time after six months from the date of the most recent disposition made in respect of the offence or, with leave of a youth court judge, at any earlier time, and, where the youth court is satisfied that there are grounds for the review under subsection (4), the court shall review the disposition. *Optional review of disposition involving custody*

(4) A disposition made in respect of a young person may be reviewed under subsection (3) *Grounds for review under subsection (3)*

(a) on the ground that the young person has made sufficient progress to justify a change in disposition;
(b) on the ground that the circumstances that led to the committal to custody have changed materially;
(c) on the ground that new services or programs are available that were not available at the time of the disposition; or
(d) on such other grounds as the youth court considers appropriate.

No review where appeal pending

(5) No review of a disposition in respect of which an appeal has been taken shall be made under this section until all proceedings in respect of any such appeal have been completed.

Youth court may order appearance of young person for review

(6) Where a provincial director is required under subsections (1) to (3) to cause a young person to be brought before the youth court and fails to do so, the youth court may, on application made by the young person, his parent or the Attorney General or his agent, or on its own motion, order the provincial director to cause the young person to be brought before the youth court.

Progress report

(7) The youth court shall, before reviewing under this section a disposition made in respect of a young person, require the provincial director to cause to be prepared, and to submit to the youth court, a progress report on the performance of the young person since the disposition took effect.

Additional information in progress report

(8) A person preparing a progress report in respect of a young person may include in the report such information relating to the personal and family history and present environment of the young person as he considers advisable.

Written or oral report

(9) A progress report shall be in writing unless it cannot reasonably be committed to writing, in which case it may, with leave of the youth court, be submitted orally in court.

Provisions of subsections 14(4) to (10) to apply

(10) The provisions of subsections 14(4) to (10) apply, with such modifications as the circumstances require, in respect of progress reports.

Notice of review from provincial director

(11) Where a disposition made in respect of a young person is to be reviewed under subsection (1) or (2), the provincial director shall cause such notice as may be directed by rules of court applicable to the youth court or, in the absence of such direction, at least five clear days' notice of the review to be given in writing to the young person, his parents and the Attorney General or his agent.

Notice of review from person requesting it

(12) Where a review of a disposition made in respect of a young person is requested under subsection (3), the person requesting the review shall cause such notice as may be directed by rules of court applicable to the youth court or, in the absence of such direction, at least five clear days' notice of the review to be given in writing to the young person, his parents and the Attorney General or his agent.

(13) Any notice given to a parent under subsection (11) or (12) shall include a statement that the young person whose disposition is to be reviewed has the right to be represented by counsel.

Statement of right to counsel

(14) A notice under subsection (11) or (12) may be served personally or may be sent by registered mail. 1986, c. 32, s. 21(1).

Service of notice

(15) Any of the persons entitled to notice under subsection (11) or (12) may waive the right to such notice.

Notice may be waived

(16) Where notice under subsection (11) or (12) is not given in accordance with this section, the youth court may
  (a) adjourn the proceedings and order that the notice be given in such manner and to such person as it directs; or
  (b) dispense with the notice where, in the opinion of the court, having regard to the circumstances, notice may be dispensed with.

Where notice not given

(17) Where a youth court reviews under this section a disposition made in respect of a young person, it may, after affording the young person, his parent, the Attorney General or his agent and the provincial director an opportunity to be heard, having regard to the needs of the young person and the interests of society.
  (a) confirm the disposition;
  (b) where the young person is in secure custody, by order direct that the young person be placed in open custody; or
  (c) release the young person from custody and place him on probation in accordance with section 23 for a period not exceeding the remainder of the period for which he was committed to custody.
1986, c. 32, s. 21(2).

Decision of the youth court after review

(18) Repealed. 1986, c. 32, s. 21(3), effective September 1, 1986. 1986, c. 32, s. 21.

Form of disposition

29. (1) Where a young person is held in custody pursuant to a disposition, the provincial director may, if he is satisfied that the needs of the young person and the interests of society would be better served thereby, cause notice in writing to be given to the young person, his parent and the Attorney General or his agent that he recommends that the young person
  (a) be transferred from a place or facility of secure custody to a place or facility of open custody, or
  (b) be released from custody and placed on probation,
and give a copy of the notice to the youth court. 1986, c. 32, s. 22(1).

Recommendation of provincial director for transfer to open custody or for probation

(1.1) The provincial director shall include in any notice given under subsection (1) the reasons for his recommendation and, in the case of a recommendation that the

Contents of notice

young person be placed on probation, the conditions that he would recommend be attached to a probation order. 1986, c. 32, s. 22(1).

Application to court for review of recommendation

(2) Where notice of a recommendation is made under subsection (1) with respect to a disposition made in respect of a young person, the youth court shall, if an application for review is made by the young person, his parent or the Attorney General or his agent within ten days after service of the notice, forthwith review the disposition. 1986, c. 32, s. 22(1).

Subsections 28(5), (7) to (10) and (12) to (18) apply

(3) Subsections 28(5), (7) to (10) and (12) to (18) apply with such modifications as the circumstances require, in respect of reviews made under this section and any notice required under subsection 28(12) shall be given to the provincial director.

Where no application for review made under subsection (2)

(4) A youth court that receives a notice under subsection (1) shall, if no application for a review is made under subsection (2),

(a) in the case of a recommendation that a young person be transferred from a place or facility of secure custody to a place or facility of open custody, order that the young person be so transferred;

(b) in the case of a recommendation that a young person be released from custody and placed on probation, release the young person and place him on probation in accordance with section 23; or

(c) where the court deems it advisable, make no direction under this subsection.

1986, c. 32, s. 22(2).

Conditions in probation order

(4.1) Where the youth court places a young person on probation pursuant to paragraph (4)(b), the court shall include in the probation order such conditions referred to in section 23 as it considers advisable, having regard to the recommendations of the provincial director. 1986, c. 32, s. 22(2).

Notice where no direction made

(4.2) Where a youth court, pursuant to paragraph (4)(c), makes no direction under subsection (4), it shall forthwith cause a notice of its decision to be given to the provincial director. 1986, c. 32, s. 22(2).

Provincial director may request review

(4.3) Where the provincial director is given a notice under subsection (4.2), he may request a review under this section. 1986, c. 32, s. 22(2).

Where the provincial director requests a review

(5) Where the provincial director requests a review pursuant to subsection (4.3).

(a) the provincial director shall cause such notice as may be directed by rules of court applicable to the youth court or, in the absence of such direction, at least five clear days notice of the review to be given in writing to the young person, his parents and the Attorney General or his agent; and

(b) the youth court shall forthwith, after the notice required under paragraph (a) is given, review the disposition.

1986, c. 32, s. 22(3).

(6) Repealed. 1986, c. 32, s. 22(4), effective September 1, 1986. 1986, c. 32, s. 22.

Form of notice

30. (1) Where a review board is established or designated by a province for the purposes of this section, that board shall, subject to this section, carry out in that province the duties and functions of a youth court under sections 28 and 29 other than releasing a young person from custody and placing him on probation.

Review board

(2) Subject to this Act, a review board may carry out any duties or functions that are assigned to it by the province that established or designated it.

Other duties of review board

(3) Where a review board is established or designated by a province for the purposes of this section, the provincial director shall at the same time as any notice is given under subsection 29(1) cause a copy of the notice to be given to the review board.

Notice under section 29

(4) A review board shall cause notice of any decision made by it in respect of a young person pursuant to section 28 or 29 to be given forthwith in writing to the young person, his parents, the Attorney General or his agent and the provincial director, and a copy of the notice to be given to the youth court.

Notice of decision of review board

(5) Subject to subsection (6), any decision of a review board under this section shall take effect ten days after the decision is made unless an application for review is made under section 31.

Decision of review board to take effect where no review

(6) Where a review board decides that a young person should be released from custody and placed on probation, it shall so recommend to the youth court and, if no application for a review of the decision is made under section 31, the youth court shall forthwith on the expiration of the ten day period referred to in subsection (5) release the young person from custody and place him on probation in accordance with section 23, and shall include in the probation order such conditions referred to in that section as the court considers advisable having regard to the recommendations of the review board.

Decision respecting release from custody and probation

(7) Repealed. 1986, c. 32, s. 23, effective September 1, 1986. 1986, c. 32, s. 23.

Form of notice of decision of review board

31. (1) Where the review board reviews a disposition under section 30, the youth court shall, on the application of the young person in respect of whom the review

Review by youth court

was made, his parents, the Attorney General or his agent or the provincial director, made within ten days after the decision of the review board is made, forthwith review the decision.

Subsections 28(5), (7) to (10) and (12) to (18) apply

(2) Subsections 28(5), (7) to (10) and (12) to (18) apply, with such modifications as the circumstances require, in respect of reviews made under this section and any notice required under subsection 28(12) shall be given to the provincial director.

Review of dispositions not involving custody

32. (1) Where a youth court has made any disposition in respect of a young person, other than or in addition to a disposition under paragraph 20(1)(k), the youth court shall, on the application of the young person, his parent, the Attorney General or his agent or the provincial director, made at any time after six months from the date of the disposition or, with leave of a youth court judge, at any earlier time, review the disposition if the court is satisfied that there are grounds for a review under subsection (2). 1986, c. 32, s. 24(1).

Grounds for review

(2) A review of a disposition may be made under this section
 (a) on the ground that the circumstances that led to the disposition have changed materially;
 (b) on the ground that the young person in respect of whom the review is to be made is unable to comply with or is experiencing serious difficulty in complying with the terms of the disposition;
 (c) on the ground that the terms of the disposition are adversely affecting the opportunities available to the young person to obtain services, education or employment or
 (d) on such other grounds as the youth court considers appropriate.

Progress report

(3) The youth court may, before reviewing under this section a disposition made in respect of a young person, require the provincial director to cause to be prepared, and to submit to the youth court, a progress report on the performance of the young person since the disposition took effect.

Subsections 28(8) to (10) apply

(4) Subsections 28(8) to (10) apply, with such modifications as the circumstances require, in respect of any progress report required under subsection (3).

Subsections 28(5) and (12) to (16) apply

(5) Subsections 28(5) and (12) to (16) apply, with such modifications as the circumstances require, in respect of reviews made under this section and any notice required under subsection 28(12) shall be given to the provincial director.

Compelling appearance of young person

(6) The youth court may, by summons or warrant, compel a young person in respect of whom a review is to be made under this section to appear before the youth court for the purposes of the review.

(7) Where a youth court reviews under this section a disposition made in respect of a young person, it may, after affording the young person, his parent, the Attorney General or his agent and the provincial director an opportunity to be heard,
> (a) confirm the disposition;
> (b) terminate the disposition and discharge the young person from any further obligation of the disposition; or
> (c) vary the disposition or make such new disposition listed in section 20, other than a committal to custody, for such period of time, not exceeding the remainder of the period of the earlier disposition, as the court deems appropriate in the circumstances of the case.

1986, c. 32, s. 24(2).

(8) Subject to subsection (9), where a disposition made in respect of a young person is reviewed under this section, no disposition made under subsection (7) shall, without the consent of the young person, be more onerous than the remaining portion of the disposition reviewed.

(9) A youth court may under this section extend the time within which a disposition made under paragraphs 20(1)(b) to (g) is to be complied with by a young person where the court is satisfied that the young person requires more time to comply with the disposition, but in no case shall the extension be for a period of time that expires more than twelve months after the date the disposition would otherwise have expired. 1986, c. 32, s. 24(3). 1986, c. 32, s. 24.

Decision of the youth court after review

New disposition not to be more onerous

Exception

33. Repealed. 1986, c. 32, s. 25, effective September 1, 1986.

Review of disposition where failure to comply

34. Subject to sections 28 to 32, subsections 20(2) to (8) and sections 21 to 25.1 apply, with such modifications as the circumstances require, in respect of dispositions made under sections 28 to 32. 1986, c. 32, s. 25.

Sections 20 to 26 apply to dispositions on review

Temporary Release from Custody

35. (1) The provincial director of a province may, subject to any terms or conditions that he considers desirable, authorize a young person committed to custody in the province pursuant to a disposition made under this Act
> (a) to be temporarily released for a period not exceeding fifteen days where, in his opinion, it is necessary or desirable that the young person be absent, with or without escort, for medical, compassionate or humanitarian reasons or for the purpose of rehabilitating the young person or re-integrating him into the community; or

Temporary absence or day release

(b) to be released from custody on such days and during such hours as he specifies in order that the young person may
  (i) attend school or any other educational or training institution,
  (ii) obtain or continue employment or perform domestic or other duties required by the young person's family, or
  (iii) participate in a program specified by him that, in his opinion, will enable the young person to better carry out his employment or improve his education or training.
1986, c. 32, s. 26(1).

Limitation

(2) A young person who is released from custody pursuant to subsection (1) shall be released only for such periods of time as are necessary to attain the purpose for which the young person is released.

Revocation of authorization for release

(3) The provincial director of a province may, at any time, revoke an authorization made under subsection (1). 1986, c. 32, s. 26(2).

Arrest and return to custody

(4) Where the provincial director or his delegate revokes an authorization for a young person to be released from custody under subsection (3) or where a young person fails to comply with any term or condition of his release from custody under this section, the young person may be arrested without warrant and returned to custody.

Prohibition

(5) A young person who has been committed to custody under this Act shall not be released from custody before the expiration of the period of his custody except in accordance with subsection (1) unless the release is ordered under sections 28 to 32 or otherwise according to law by a court of competent jurisdiction. 1986, c. 32, s. 26(3). 1986, c. 32, s. 26.

Effect of Termination of Disposition

Effect of absolute discharge or termination of dispositions

36. (1) Subject to section 12 of the *Canada Evidence Act*, where a young person is found guilty of an offence, and
  (a) a youth court directs under paragraph 20(1)(a) that the young person be discharged absolutely, or
  (b) all the dispositions made under this Act in respect of the offence have ceased to have effect,
the young person shall be deemed not to have been found guilty or convicted of the offence except that,
  (c) the young person may plead *autrefois convict* in respect of any subsequent charge relating to the offence;
  (d) a youth court may consider the finding of guilt in considering an application for a transfer to ordinary court under section 16;

(e) any court or justice may consider the finding of guilt in considering an application for judicial interim release or in considering what dispositions to make or sentence to impose for any offence; and
(f) the National Parole Board or any provincial parole board may consider the finding of guilt in considering an application for parole or pardon. 1986, c. 32, s. 27.

(2) For greater certainty and without restricting the generality of subsection (1), an absolute discharge under paragraph 20(1)(a) or the termination of all dispositions in respect of an offence for which a young person is found guilty removes any disqualification in respect of the offence to which the young person is subject pursuant to any Act of Parliament by reason of a conviction.

Disqualifications removed

(3) No application form for or relating to
(a) employment in any department, as defined in section 2 of the *Financial Administration Act*,
(b) employment by any Crown corporation as defined in section 95 of the *Financial Administration Act*,
(c) enrolment in the Canadian Forces, or
(d) employment on or in connection with the operation of any work, undertaking or business that is within the legislative authority of the Parliament of Canada,

shall contain any question that by its terms requires the applicant to disclose that he has been charged with or found guilty of an offence in respect of which he has, under this Act, been discharged absolutely or has completed all the dispositions. 1983-84, c. 31, s. 13.

Applications for employment

(4) Any person who uses or authorizes the use of an application form in contravention of subsection (3) is guilty of an offence punishable on summary conviction.

Punishment

(5) A finding of guilt under this Act is not a previous conviction for the purposes of any offence under any Act of Parliament for which a greater punishment is prescribed by reason of previous convictions. 1983-84, c. 31, s. 13; 1986, c. 32, s. 27.

Finding of guilt not a previous conviction

Youth Workers

37. The duties and functions of a youth worker in respect of a young person whose case has been assigned to him by the provincial director include
(a) where the young person is bound by a probation order that requires him to be under supervision, supervising the young person in complying with the conditions of the probation order or in carrying out any other disposition made together with it;
(b) where the young person is found guilty of an offence, giving such assistance to him as he

Duties of youth worker

considers appropriate up to the time the young person is discharged or the disposition of his case terminates;
   (c) attending court when he considers it advisable or when required by the youth court to be present;
   (d) preparing, at the request of the provincial director, a pre-disposition report or a progress report; and
   (e) performing such other duties and functions as the provincial director requires.
1986, c. 32, s. 28.

Protection of Privacy of Young Persons

Identity not to be published

38. (1) Subject to this section, no person shall publish by any means any report
   (a) of an offence committed or alleged to have been committed by a young person, unless an order has been made under section 16 with respect thereto, or
   (b) of a hearing, adjudication, disposition or appeal concerning a young person who committed or is alleged to have committed an offence
in which the name of the young person, a child or a young person who is a victim of the offence or a child or a young person who appeared as a witness in connection with the offence, or in which any information serving to identify such young person or child, is disclosed. 1986, c. 32, ss. 29(1), (2).

Limitation

(1.1) Subsection (1) does not apply in respect of the disclosure of information in the course of the administration of justice where it is not the purpose of the disclosure to make the information known in the community. 1986, c. 32, s. 29(3).

Ex parte application for leave to publish

(1.2) A youth court judge shall, on the *ex parte* application of a peace officer, make an order permitting any person to publish a report described in subsection (1) that contains the name of a young person, or information serving to identify a young person, who has committed or is alleged to have committed an indictable offence, if the judge is satisfied that
   (a) there is reason to believe that the young person is dangerous to others; and
   (b) publication of the report is necessary to assist in apprehending the young person.
1986, c. 32, s. 29(3).

Order ceases to have effect

(1.3) An order made under subsection (1.2) shall cease to have effect two days after it is made. 1986, c. 32, s. 29(3).

Application for leave to publish

(1.4) The youth court may, on the application of any person referred to in subsection (1), make an order permitting any person to publish a report in which the name of that person, or information serving to identify that person, would be disclosed, if the court is satisfied that the publication of the report would not be contrary to the best interests of that person. 1986, c. 32, s. 29(3).

(2) Every one who contravenes subsection (1) *Contravention*
  (a) is guilty of an indictable offence and is liable to imprisonment for not more than two years; or
  (b) is guilty of an offence punishable on summary conviction.

(3) Where an accused is charged with an offence under paragraph (2)(a), a provincial court judge has absolute jurisdiction to try the case and his jurisdiction does not depend on the consent of the accused. 1986, c. 32, s. 29(3). *Provincial court judge has absolute jurisdiction on indictment*

39. (1) Subject to subsection (2), where a court or justice before whom proceedings are carried out under this Act is of the opinion *Exclusion from hearing*
  (a) that any evidence or information presented to the court or justice would be seriously injurious or seriously prejudicial to
    (i) the young person who is being dealt with in the proceedings,
    (ii) a child or young person who is a witness in the proceedings,
    (iii) a child or young person who is aggrieved by or the victim of the offence charged in the proceedings, or
  (b) that it would be in the interest of public morals, the maintenance of order or the proper administration of justice to exclude any or all members of the public from the court room,
the court or justice may exclude any person from all or part of the proceedings if the court or justice deems that person's presence to be unnecessary to the conduct of the proceedings.

(2) Subject to section 577 of the *Criminal Code* and except where it is necessary for the purposes of subsection 13(6) of this Act, a court or justice may not, pursuant to subsection (1), exclude from proceedings under this Act *Exception*
  (a) the prosecutor;
  (b) the young person who is being dealt with in the proceedings, his parent, his counsel or any adult assisting him pursuant to subsection 11(7);
  (c) the provincial director or his agent; or
  (d) the youth worker to whom the young person's case has been assigned.
1986, c. 32, s. 30(1).

(3) The youth court, after it has found a young person guilty of an offence, or the youth court or the review board, during a review of a disposition under sections 28 *Exclusion after adjudication or during review*

to 32, may, in its discretion, exclude from the court or from a hearing of the review board, as the case may be, any person other than
  (a) the young person or his counsel,
  (b) the provincial director or his agent,
  (c) the youth worker to whom the young person's case has been assigned, and
  (d) the Attorney General or his agent,
when any information is being presented to the court or the review board the knowledge of which might, in the opinion of the court or review board, be seriously injurious or seriously prejudicial to the young person. 1986, c. 32, s. 30(2).

Exception

(4) The exception set out in paragraph (3)(a) is subject to subsection 13(6) of this Act and section 577 of the *Criminal Code*. 1986, c. 32, s. 30(3). 1986, c. 32, s. 30.

Records that May Be Kept

Youth court, review board and other courts

40. (1) A youth court, review board or any court dealing with matters arising out of proceedings under this Act may keep a record of any case arising under this Act that comes before it.

Exception

(2) For greater certainty, this section does not apply in respect of proceedings held in ordinary court pursuant to an order under section 16.

Records in central repository

41. (1) A record of any offence of which a young person has been found guilty under this Act may be kept in such central repository as the Commissioner of the Royal Canadian Mounted Police may, from time to time, designate for the purpose of keeping criminal history files or records on offenders or keeping records for the identification of offenders.

Police force to provide record

(2) Where a young person is found guilty of an offence under this Act, the police force responsible for the investigation of the offence shall provide a record of the offence, including the original or a copy of any fingerprints or photographs of the young person taken by or on behalf of the police force, for inclusion in any central repository designated pursuant to subsection (1).

Police records

42. A record relating to any offence alleged to have been committed by a young person, including the original or a copy of any fingerprints or photographs of the young person, may be kept by any police force responsible for, or participating in, the investigation of the offence.

Government records

43. (1) A department or agency of any government in Canada may keep records containing information obtained by the department or agency

(a) for the purposes of an investigation of an offence alleged to have been committed by a young person;
(b) for use in proceedings against a young person under this Act;
(c) for the purpose of administering a disposition;
(d) for the purpose of considering whether, instead of commencing or continuing judicial proceedings under this Act against a young person, to use alternative measures to deal with the young person; or
(e) as a result of the use of alternative measures to deal with a young person.

(2) Any person or organization may keep records containing information obtained by the person or organization   *Private records*
(a) as a result of the use of alternative measures to deal with a young person alleged to have committed an offence; or
(b) for the purpose of administering or participating in the administration of a disposition.

Fingerprints and Photographs

44. (1) Subject to this section, the *Identification of Criminals Act* applies in respect of young persons.   *Identification of Criminals Act applies*

(2) No fingerprints or photograph of a young person who is accused of committing an offence shall be taken except in the circumstances in which an adult may, under the *Identification of Criminals Act*, be subjected to the measurements, processes and operations referred to in that Act.   *Limitation*

Disclosure of Records

44.1 (1) Subject to subsection (2), any record that is kept pursuant to section 40 shall, and any record that is kept pursuant to sections 41 to 43 may, on request, be made available for inspection to   *Records made available*
(a) the young person to whom the record relates;
(b) counsel acting on behalf of the young person;
(c) the Attorney General or his agent;
(d) a parent of the young person or any adult assisting the young person pursuant to subsection 11(7), during the course of any proceedings relating to the offence or alleged offence to which the record relates or during the term of any disposition made in respect of the offence;
(e) any judge, court or review board, for any purpose relating to proceedings relating to the young person under this Act or to proceedings in ordinary court in respect of offences committed or alleged to have been committed by the young person, whether as a young person or an adult;
(f) any peace officer,

(i) for the purpose of investigating any offence that the young person is suspected of having committed, or in respect of which the young person has been arrested or charged, whether as a young person or an adult, or

(ii) for any purpose related to the administration of the case to which the record relates during the course of proceedings against the young person or the term of any disposition;

(g) any member of a department or agency of a government in Canada, or any agent thereof, that is

(i) engaged in the administration of alternative measures in respect of the young person,

(ii) preparing a report in respect of the young person pursuant to this Act or for the purpose of assisting a court in sentencing the young person after he becomes an adult or is transferred to ordinary court pursuant to section 16,

(iii) engaged in the supervision or care of the young person, whether as a young person or an adult, or in the administration of a disposition or a sentence in respect of the young person, whether as a young person or an adult, or

(iv) considering an application for parole or pardon made by the young person after he becomes an adult;

(h) any person, or person within a class of persons, designated by the Governor in Council, or the Lieutenant Governor in Council of a province, for a purpose and to the extent specified by the Governor in Council or the Lieutenant Governor in Council, as the case may be;

(i) any person, for the purpose of determining whether to grant security clearances required by the Government of Canada or the government of a province or a municipality for purposes of employment or the performance of services;

(j) any employee or agent of the Government of Canada, for statistical purposes pursuant to the *Statistics Act*; and

(k) any other person who is deemed, or any person within a class of persons that is deemed, by a youth court judge to have a valid interest in the record, to the extent directed by the judge, if the judge is satisfied that the disclosure is

(i) desirable in the public interest for research or statistical purposes, or

(ii) desirable in the interest of the proper administration of justice.

(2) Where a youth court has withheld the whole or a part of a report from any person pursuant to subsection 13(6) or 14(7), the report or part thereof shall not be made available to that person for inspection under subsection (1). *Exception*

(3) Nothing in paragraph (1)(e) authorizes the introduction into evidence of any part of a record that would not otherwise be admissible in evidence. *Introduction into evidence*

(4) Where a record is made available for inspection to any person under paragraph (1)(j) or subparagraph (1)(k)(i), that person may subsequently disclose information contained in the record, but may not disclose the information in any form that would reasonably be expected to identify the young person to whom it relates. *Disclosures for research or statistical purposes*

(5) Any record that is kept pursuant to sections 40 to 43 may, on request, be made available for inspection to the victim of the offence to which the record relates. *Record made available to victim*

(6) Any person to whom a record is required or authorized to be made available for inspection under this section may be given any information contained in the record and may be given a copy of any part of the record. *Disclosure of information and copies of records*

44.2 (1) A peace officer may disclose to any person any information in a record kept pursuant to section 42 that it is necessary to disclose in the conduct of the investigation of an offence. *Disclosure by peace officer during investigation*

(2) A peace officer may disclose to an insurance company information in any record that is kept pursuant to section 42 for the purpose of investigating any claim arising out of an offence committed or alleged to have been committed by the young person to whom the record relates. *Disclosure to insurance company*

Non-Disclosure and Destruction of Records

45. (1) Subject to sections 45.1 and 45.2, records kept pursuant to sections 40 to 43 may not be made available for inspection under section 44.1 or 44.2 in the following circumstances: *Non-disclosure*

(a) where the young person to whom the record relates is charged with the offence to which the record relates and is acquitted otherwise than by reason of insanity, on the expiration of two months after the expiration of the time allowed for the taking of an appeal or, where an appeal is taken, on the expiration of three months after all proceedings in respect of the appeal have been completed;

(b) where the charge against the young person is dismissed for any reason other than acquittal or withdrawn, on the expiration of one year after the dismissal or withdrawal;

(c) where the charge against the young person is stayed, with no proceedings being taken against the young person for a period of one year, on the expiration of the one year;

(d) where alternative measures are used to deal with the young person, on the expiration of two years after the young person consents to participate in the alternative measures in accordance with paragraph 4(1)(c);
(e) where the young person is found guilty of the offence and it is a summary conviction offence, on the expiration of five years after the young person is found guilty; and
(f) where the young person is found guilty of the offence and it is an indictable offence, on the expiration of five years after all dispositions made in respect of that offence and all dispositions made in respect of any other indictable offence of which the young person may have been found guilty after he was found guilty of that offence but prior to the expiration of the five year period have been completed.

Record in central repository to be destroyed

(2) Any record kept pursuant to section 41 shall be destroyed forthwith when the circumstances set out in subsection (1) are realized in respect of that record.

Other records may be destroyed

(3) Any record kept pursuant to sections 40 to 43 may, in the discretion of the person or body keeping the record, be destroyed at any time before or after the circumstances set out in subsection (1) are realized in respect of that record.

Young person deemed not to have committed offence

(4) A young person shall be deemed not to have committed any offence to which a record kept pursuant to sections 40 to 43 relates when the circumstances set out in paragraphs (1)(d), (e) or (f) are realized in respect of that record.

Deemed election

(5) For the purposes of paragraphs (1)(e) and (f), where no election is made in respect of an offence that may be prosecuted by indictment or proceeded with by way of summary conviction, the Attorney General or his agent shall be deemed to have elected to proceed with the offence as an offence punishable on summary conviction.

Application to delinquency

(6) This section applies, with such modifications as the circumstances require, in respect of records relating to the offence of delinquency under the *Juvenile Delinquents Act* as it read immediately prior to April 2, 1984.

Where records may be made available

45.1 (1) A youth court judge may, on application by any person, order that any record to which subsection 45(1) applies, or any part thereof, be made available for inspection to that person or a copy of the record or part thereof be given to that person, if a youth court judge is satisfied that
(a) that person has a valid and substantial interest in the record or part thereof;
(b) it is necessary for the record, part thereof or copy thereof to be made available in the interest of the proper administration of justice; and

(c) disclosure of the record or part thereof or information is not prohibited under any other Act of Parliament or the legislature of a province.

(2) An application under subsection (1) in respect of a record shall not be heard unless the person who makes the application has given the young person to whom the record relates and the person or body that has possession of the record at least five days notice in writing of the application and the young person and the person or body that has possession has had a reasonable opportunity to be heard. Notice

(3) In any order under subsection (1), the youth court judge shall set out the purposes for which the record may be used. Use of record

45.2 Where records originally kept pursuant to sections 40, 42 or 43 are in the possession of the Dominion Archivist or the archivist for any province, that person may disclose any information contained in the record to any other person if Records in the possession of archivist

(a) the Attorney General or his agent is satisfied that the disclosure is desirable in the public interest for research or statistical purposes; and

(b) the person to whom the information is disclosed undertakes not to disclose the information in any form that could reasonably be expected to identify the young person to whom it relates.

46. (1) Except as authorized or required by this Act, no record kept pursuant to sections 40 to 43 may be made available for inspection, and no copy, print or negative thereof or information contained therein may be given, to any person where to do so would serve to identify the young person to whom it relates as a young person dealt with under this Act. Prohibition against disclosure

(2) No person who is employed in keeping or maintaining records referred to in subsection (1) is restricted from doing anything prohibited under subsection (1) with respect to any other person so employed. Exception for employees

(3) Subject to section 45.1, no record kept pursuant to sections 40 to 43, and no copy, print or negative thereof, may be used for any purpose that would serve to identify the young person to whom the record relates as a young person dealt with under this Act after the circumstances set out in subsection 45(1) are realized in respect of that record. Prohibition against use

(4) Any person who fails to comply with this section or subsection 45(2) Offence

(a) is guilty of an indictable offence and liable to imprisonment for two years; or

(5) The jurisdiction of a provincial court judge to try an accused is absolute and does not depend on the consent of the accused where the accused is charged with an offence under paragraph (4)(a). Absolute jurisdiction of provincial court judge

Contempt of Court

47. (1) Every youth court has the same power, jurisdiction and authority to deal with and impose punishment for contempt against the court as may be exercised by the superior court of criminal jurisdiction of the province in which the court is situated.

Contempt against youth court

(2) The youth court has exclusive jurisdiction in respect of every contempt of court committed by a young person against the youth court whether or not committed in the face of the court and every contempt of court committed by a young person against any other court otherwise than in the face of that court.

Exclusive jurisdiction of youth court

(3) The youth court has jurisdiction in respect of every contempt of court committed by a young person against any other court in the face of that court and every contempt of court committed by an adult against the youth court in the face of the youth court, but nothing in this subsection affects the power, jurisdiction or authority of any other court to deal with or impose punishment for contempt of court.

Concurrent jurisdiction of youth court

(4) Where a youth court or any other court finds a young person guilty of contempt of court, it may make any one of the dispositions set out in section 20, or any number thereof that are not inconsistent with each other, but no other disposition or sentence.

Dispositions

(5) Section 636 of the *Criminal Code* applies in respect of proceedings under this section in youth court against adults, with such modifications as the circumstances require.

Section 636 of Criminal Code applies in respect of adults

(6) A finding of guilt under this section for contempt of court or a disposition or sentence made in respect thereof may be appealed as if the finding were a conviction or the disposition or sentence were a sentence in a prosecution by indictment in ordinary court.

Appeals

Forfeiture of Recognizances

48. Applications for the forfeiture of recognizances of young persons shall be made to the youth court.

Applications for forfeiture of recognizances

49. (1) Where a recognizance binding a young person has been endorsed with a certificate pursuant to subsection 704(1) of the *Criminal Code*, a youth court judge shall,

Proceedings in case of default

(a) on the request of the Attorney General or his agent, fix a time and place for the hearing of an application for the forfeiture of the recognizance; and

(b) after fixing a time and place for the hearing, cause to be sent by registered mail, not less than ten days before the time so fixed, to each principal and surety named in the recognizance, directed to him at his latest known address, a notice requiring him to appear at the time and place fixed by the judge to show cause why the recognizance should not be forfeited.

(2) Where subsection (1) is complied with, the youth court judge may, after giving the parties an opportunity to be heard, in his discretion grant or refuse the application and make any order with respect to the forfeiture of the recognizance that he considers proper.

(3) Where, pursuant to subsection (2), a youth court judge orders forfeiture of a recognizance, the principal and his sureties become judgment debtors of the Crown, each in the amount that the judge orders him to pay.

(4) An order made under subsection (2) may be filed with the clerk of the superior court or, in the province of Quebec, the prothonotary and, where an order is filed, the clerk or the prothonotary shall issue a writ of *fieri facias* in Form 30 set out in the *Criminal Code* and deliver it to the sheriff of each of the territorial divisions in which any of the principal and his sureties resides, carries on business or has property.

(5) Where a deposit has been made by a person against whom an order for forfeiture of a recognizance has been made, no writ of *fieri facias* shall issue, but the amount of the deposit shall be transferred by the person who has custody of it to the person who is entitled by law to receive it.

(6) Subsections 704(2) and (4) of the *Criminal Code* do not apply in respect of proceedings under this Act.

(7) Sections 706 and 707 of the *Criminal Code* apply in respect of writs of *fieri facias* issued pursuant to this section as if they were issued pursuant to section 705 of the *Criminal Code*.

Order for forfeiture of recognizance

Judgment debtors of the Crown

Order may be filed

Where a deposit has been made

Subsections 704(2) and (4) of Criminal Code do not apply

Sections 706 and 707 of Criminal Code apply

Interference with Dispositions

50. (1) Every one who
(a) induces or assists a young person to leave unlawfully a place of custody or other place in which the young person has been placed pursuant to a disposition,
(b) unlawfully removes a young person from a place referred to in paragraph (a),
(c) knowingly harbours or conceals a young person who has unlawfully left a place referred to in paragraph (a),
(d) wilfully induces or assists a young person to breach or disobey a term or condition of a disposition, or
(e) wilfully prevents or interferes with the performance by a young person of a term or condition of a disposition

Inducing a young person, etc.

is guilty of an indictable offence and is liable to imprisonment for two years or is guilty of an offence punishable on summary conviction.

(2) The jurisdiction of a provincial court judge to try an adult accused of an indictable offence under this section is absolute and does not depend on the consent of the accused. 1986, c. 32, s. 37. 1986, c. 32, s. 37.

Absolute jurisdiction of provincial court judge

Application of the Criminal Code

51. Except to the extent that they are inconsistent with or excluded by this Act, all the provisions of the *Criminal Code* apply, with such modifications as the circumstances require, in respect of offences alleged to have been committed by young persons.

Application of Criminal Code

Procedure

52. (1) Subject to this section and except to the extent that they are inconsistent with this Act,
  (a) the provisions of Part XXIV of the *Criminal Code*, and
  (b) any other provisions of the *Criminal Code* that apply in respect of summary conviction offences and relate to trial proceedings
apply to proceedings under this Act
  (c) in respect of a summary conviction offence, and
  (d) in respect of an indictable offence as if it were defined in the enactment creating it as a summary conviction offence.

Part XXIV and summary conviction trial provisions of Criminal Code to apply

(2) For greater certainty and notwithstanding subsection (1) or any other provision of this Act, an indictable offence committed by a young person is, for the purposes of this or any other Act, an indictable offence.

Indictable offences

(3) Section 577 of the *Criminal Code* applies in respect of proceedings under this Act, whether the proceedings relate to an indictable offence or an offence punishable on summary conviction.

Attendance of young person

(4) In proceedings under this Act, subsection 721(2) of the *Criminal Code* does not apply in respect of an indictable offence.

Limitation period

(5) Section 744 of the *Criminal Code* does not apply in respect of proceedings under this Act.

Costs

53. Indictable offences and offences punishable on summary conviction may under this Act be charged in the same information and tried jointly.

Counts charged in information

54. (1) Where a person is required to attend to give evidence before a youth court, the subpoena directed to that person may be issued by a youth court judge, whether or not the person whose attendance is required is within the same province as the youth court.

Issue of subpoena

(2) A subpoena issued by a youth court and directed to a person who is not within the same province as the youth court shall be served personally on the person to whom it is directed.

55. A warrant that is issued out of a youth court may be executed anywhere in Canada. Warrant

Evidence

56. (1) Subject to this section, the law relating to the admissibility of statements made by persons accused of committing offences applies in respect of young persons. General law on admissibility of statements to apply

(2) No oral or written statement given by a young person to a peace officer or other person who is, in law, a person in authority is admissible against the young person unless When statements are admissible
 (a) the statement was voluntary;
 (b) the person to whom the statement was given has, before the statement was made, clearly explained to the young person, in language appropriate to his age and understanding, that
  (i) the young person is under no obligation to give a statement,
  (ii) any statement given by him may be used as evidence in proceedings against him,
  (iii) the young person has the right to consult another person in accordance with paragraph (c), and
  (iv) any statement made by the young person is required to be made in the presence of the person consulted, unless the young person desires otherwise;
 (c) the young person has, before the statement was made, been given a reasonable opportunity to consult with counsel or a parent, or in the absence of a parent, an adult relative, or in the absence of a parent and an adult relative, any other appropriate adult chosen by the young person; and
 (d) where the young person consults any person pursuant to paragraph (c), the young person has been given a reasonable opportunity to make the statement in the presence of that person.

(3) The requirements set out in paragraphs (2)(b), (c) and (d) do not apply in respect of oral statements where they are made spontaneously by the young person to a peace officer or other person in authority before that person has had a reasonable opportunity to comply with those requirements. Exception in certain cases for oral statements

(4) A young person may waive his rights under paragraph (2)(c) or (d) but any such waiver shall be made in writing and shall contain a statement signed by the young person that he has been apprised of the right that he is waiving. Waiver of right to consult

Statements given under duress are inadmissible	(5) A youth court judge may rule inadmissible in any proceedings under this Act a statement given by the young person in respect of whom the proceedings are taken if the young person satisfies the judge that the statement was given under duress imposed by any person who is not, in law, a person in authority.
Parent, etc. not a person in authority	(6) For the purpose of this section, an adult consulted pursuant to paragraph 56(2)(c) shall, in the absence of evidence to the contrary, be deemed not to be a person in authority. 1986, c. 32, s. 38. 1986, c. 32, s. 38.
Testimony of a parent	**57.** (1) In any proceedings under this Act, the testimony of a parent as to the age of a person of whom he is a parent is admissible as evidence of the age of that person.
Evidence of age by certificate or record	(2) In any proceedings under this Act, (a) a birth or baptismal certificate or a copy thereof purporting to be certified under the hand of the person in whose custody such records are held is evidence of the age of the person named in the certificate or copy; and (b) an entry or record of an incorporated society that has had the control or care of the person alleged to have committed the offence in respect of which the proceedings are taken at or about the time the person came to Canada is evidence of the age of that person, if the entry or record was made before the time when the offence is alleged to have been committed.
Other evidence	(3) In the absence, before the youth court, of any certificate, copy, entry or record mentioned in subsection (2), or in corroboration of any such certificate, copy, entry or record, the youth court may receive and act upon any other information relating to age that it considers reliable.
When age may be inferred	(4) In any proceedings under this Act, the youth court may draw inferences as to the age of a person from the person's appearance or from statements made by the person in direct examination or cross-examination.
Admissions	**58.** (1) A party to any proceedings under this Act may admit any relevant fact or matter for the purpose of dispensing with proof thereof, including any fact or matter the admissibility of which depends on a ruling of law or of mixed law and fact.
Other party may adduce evidence	(2) Nothing in this section precludes a party to a proceeding from adducing evidence to prove a fact or matter admitted by another party.
Material evidence	**59.** Any evidence material to proceedings under this Act that would not but for this section be admissible in evidence may, with the consent of the parties to the

proceedings and where the young person is represented by counsel, be given in such proceedings.

60. In any proceedings under this Act where the evidence of a child or a young person is taken, it shall be taken only after the youth court judge or the justice, as the case may be, has
  (a) in all cases, if the witness is a child, and
  (b) where he deems it necessary, if the witness is a young person,
instructed the child or young person as to the duty of the witness to speak the truth and the consequences of failing to do so. 1986, c. 32, s. 39(1).

(2) Repealed. 1986, c. 32, s. 39(2), effective September 1, 1986.

(3) Repealed. 1986, c. 32, s. 39(2), effective September 1, 1986. 1986, c. 32, s. 39

Evidence of a child or young person

Solemn affirmation

Effect of evidence under solemn affirmation

61. Repealed. 1986, c. 32, s. 40, effective September 1, 1986.

Evidence of a child

62. For the purposes of this Act, service of any document may be proved by oral evidence given under oath by, or by the affidavit or statutory declaration of, the person claiming to have personally served it or sent it by mail.

Proof of service

(2) Where proof of service of any document is offered by affidavit or statutory declaration, it is not necessary to prove the signature or official character of the person making or taking the affidavit or declaration, if the official character of that person appears on the face thereof.

Proof of signature and official character unnecessary

63. It is not necessary to the validity of any information, summons, warrant, minute, disposition, conviction, order or other process or document laid, issued, filed or entered in any proceedings under this Act that any seal be attached or affixed thereto.

Seal not required

Substitution of Judges

64. (1) A youth court judge who acts in the place of another youth court judge pursuant to subsection 726(1) of the *Criminal Code* shall
  (a) if an adjudication has been made, proceed with the disposition of the case or make the order that, in the circumstances, is authorized by law; or
  (b) if no adjudication has been made, recommence the trial as if no evidence had been taken.

Powers of substitute youth court judge

(2) Where a youth court judge recommences a trial under paragraph (1)(b), he may, if the parties consent, admit into evidence a transcript of any evidence already given in the case.

Transcript of evidence already given

Functions of Clerks of Courts

Powers of clerks

65. In addition to any powers conferred on a clerk of a court by the *Criminal Code*, a clerk of the youth court may exercise such powers as are ordinarily exercised by a clerk of a court, and, in particular, may
    (a) administer oaths or affirmations in all matters relating to the business of the youth court; and
    (b) in the absence of a youth court judge, exercise all the powers of a youth court judge relating to adjournment.

Forms, Regulations and Rules of Court

Forms

66. (1) The forms set out in the schedule, varied to suit the case, or forms to the like effect, are valid and sufficient in the circumstances for which they are provided.

Where forms not provided

(2) In any case for which forms are not set out in the schedule or prescribed under section 67, the forms set out in Part XXV of the *Criminal Code*, with such modifications as the circumstances require, or other appropriate forms, may be used.

Regulations

67. The Governor in Council may make regulations
    (a) prescribing forms that may be used for purposes of this Act;
    (b) establishing uniform rules of court for youth courts across Canada, including rules regulating the practice and procedure to be followed by youth courts; and
    (c) generally for carrying out the purposes and provisions of this Act.
1986, c. 32, s. 41.

Youth court may make rules

68. (1) Every youth court for a province may, at any time with the concurrence of a majority of the judges thereof present at a meeting held for the purpose and subject to the approval of the Lieutenant Governor in Council, establish rules of court not inconsistent with this or any other Act of Parliament or with any regulations made pursuant to section 67 regulating proceedings within the jurisdiction of the youth court.

Rules of court

(2) Rules under subsection (1) may be made
    (a) generally to regulate the duties of the officers of the youth court and any other matter considered expedient to attain the ends of justice and carry into effect the provisions of this Act;
    (b) subject to any regulations made under paragraph 67(b), to regulate the practice and procedure in the youth court; and
    (c) to prescribe forms to be used in the youth court where not otherwise provided for by or pursuant to this Act.

(3) Rules of court that are made under the authority of this section shall be published in the appropriate provincial gazette.

Publication of rules

Youth Justice Committees
69. The Attorney General of a province or such other Minister as the Lieutenant Governor in Council of the province may designate, or a delegate thereof, may establish one or more committees of citizens, to be known as youth justice committees, to assist without remuneration in any aspect of the administration of this Act or in any programs or services for young offenders and may specify the method of appointment of committee members and the functions of the committees.

Youth Justice Committees

Agreements with Provinces
70. Any Minister of the Crown may, with the approval of the Governor in Council, enter into an agreement with the government of any province providing for payments by Canada to the province in respect of costs incurred by the province or a municipality for care of and services provided to young persons dealt with under this Act. 1986, c. 32, s. 42.

Agreements with provinces

Consequential Amendments

Canada Evidence Act
71. Subsection 4(2) of the *Canada Evidence Act* is repealed and the following substituted therefor:

R.S., c. E-10

"(2) The wife or husband of a person charged with an offence against subsection 50(1) of the *Young Offenders Act* or with an offence against any of sections 143 to 146, 148, 150 to 155, 157, 166 to 169, 175, 195, 197, 200, 248 to 250, 255 to 258, 289, paragraph 423(1)(c) or an attempt to commit an offence under section 146 or 155 of the *Criminal Code*, is a competent and compellable witness for the prosecution without the consent of the person charged."

Idem

Criminal Code
72. Sections 12 and 13 of the *Criminal Code* are repealed and the following substituted therefor:

R.S., c. C-34

"12. No person shall be convicted of an offence in respect of an act or omission on his part while he was under the age of twelve years."

12. Child under twelve

73. Section 441 of the said Act is repealed.

74. Subsection 442(1) of the said Act is repealed and the following substituted therefor:

1974-75-76, c. 93, s. 44

"(1) Any proceedings against an accused shall

442. Exclusion of public in certain cases	be held in open court, but where the presiding judge, magistrate or justice, as the case may be, is of the opinion that it is in the interest of public morals, the maintenance of order or the proper administration of justice to exclude all or any members of the public from the court room for all or part of the proceedings, he may so order.''

75. The said Act is further amended by adding thereto, immediately after section 660 thereof, the following section:

660.1. Transfer of young persons to place of custody	"(1) Where a young person is sentenced to imprisonment under this or any other Act of Parliament, the young person may, with the consent of the provincial director, be transferred to a place of custody for any portion of his term of imprisonment that expires before two years after the young person becomes an adult.
Removal of young person from place of custody	(2) Where the provincial director certifies that a young person transferred to a place of custody under subsection (1) can no longer be held therein without significant danger of escape or of detrimentally affecting the rehabilitation or reformation of other young persons held therein, the young person may be imprisoned during the remainder of his term of imprisonment in any place where he might, but for subsection (1), have been imprisoned.
Definitions	(3) For the purposes of this section, the expressions "young person", "provincial director" and "adult" have the meanings assigned by subsection 2(1) of the *Young Offenders Act* and the expression "place of custody" means "open custody" or "secure custody" within the meaning assigned by subsection 24(1) of that Act."

Indian Act

R.S.,c.I-6	76. Section 120 of the *Indian Act* is repealed.

Parole Act

1976-77,c.53, s. 17 (1)	77. The definition "inmate" in section 2 of the *Parole Act* is repealed and the following substituted therefor:
"inmate"	"inmate" means a person who is under a sentence of imprisonment imposed pursuant to an Act of Parliament or imposed for criminal contempt of court but does not include
	(a) a child within the meaning of the *Juvenile Delinquents Act*, as it read immediately prior to the coming into force of the *Young Offenders Act*, who is under sentence of imprisonment for an

offence known as a delinquency under the *Juvenile Delinquents Act,*
- (b) a young person within the meaning of the *Young Offenders Act* who has been committed to custody under that Act, or
- (c) a person in custody solely by reason of a sentence of imprisonment that has been ordered to be served intermittently pursuant to section 663 of the *Criminal Code.*''

Prisons and Reformatories Act

78. The definition "prisoner" in section 2 of the *Prisons and Reformatories Act* is repealed and the following substituted therefor:

"prisoner" means a person, other than
- (a) a child within the meaning of the *Juvenile Delinquents Act,* as it read immediately prior to the coming into force of the *Young Offenders Act,* with respect to whom no order pursuant to section 9 of that Act has been made, or
- (b) a young person within the meaning of the *Young Offenders Act* with respect to whom no order pursuant to section 16 of that Act has been made,

who is confined in a prison pursuant to a sentence for an offence under an Act of Parliament or any regulations made thereunder.''

1976-77,c.53, s. 45

"prisoner"

Transitional

79. (1) On and after the coming into force of this Act, no proceedings may be commenced under the *Juvenile Delinquents Act.*

(2) Where, before the coming into force of this Act, proceedings are commenced under the *Juvenile Delinquents Act* in respect of a delinquency as described in that Act alleged to have been committed by a person who was at the time of the delinquency a child as defined in that Act, the proceedings and all matters consequent thereon may be dealt with in all respects as if this Act had not come into force except that
- (a) no court may, after the coming into force of this Act, make an order under section 9 of the *Juvenile Delinquents Act* in respect of a person who in any such proceedings has been adjudged a juvenile delinquent;
- (b) where an adjudication of delinquency is made under the *Juvenile Delinquents Act,* all subsequent proceedings shall be taken under this Act as if the adjudication were a finding of guilt under section 19; and
- (c) where a disposition is made under section 20 of

Transitional

Idem

the *Juvenile Delinquents Act*, sections 28 to 32 of this Act apply in respect of the disposition as if it were made under section 20 of this Act unless the young person may, pursuant to subsection 21(1) of the *Juvenile Delinquents Act*, be dealt with under the laws of a province. 1986, c. 32, s. 43.

Idem

(3) Any person who, before the coming into force of this Act, commits an offence under a provincial statute or a by-law or ordinance of a municipality in respect of which proceedings are not commenced under the *Juvenile Delinquents Act* may be dealt with under provincial law as if the *Juvenile Delinquents Act* had not been in force when the person committed the offence.

Idem

(4) Any person who, before the coming into force of this Act, while he was a young person committed an offence in respect of which no proceedings were commenced before the coming into force of this Act may be dealt with under this Act as if the offence occurred after the coming into force of this Act.

Proceedings commence with information

(5) For the purposes of this section, proceedings are commenced by the laying of an information. 1986, c. 32, s. 43.

Repeal

Repeal

80. R.S., c 5-3 The *Juvenile Delinquents Act* is repealed.

Commencement

Commencement

81. This Act shall come into force on a day to be fixed by proclamation. (Proclaimed in force effective April 2, 1984.)

Schedule

(The Schedule to the Young Offenders Act was repealed by 1986, c. 32, s. 44, effective September 1, 1986.)

Appendix B

EXCERPTS FROM THE CRIMINAL CODE

Insanity

16. (1) No person shall be convicted of an offence in respect of an act or omission on his part while he was insane.

(2) For the purposes of this section a person is insane when he is in a state of natural imbecility or has disease of the mind to an extent that renders him incapable of appreciating the nature and quality of an act or omission or of knowing that an act or omission is wrong.

(3) A person who has specific delusions, but is in other respects sane, shall not be acquitted on the ground of insanity unless the delusions caused him to believe in the existence of a state of things that, if it existed, would have justified or excused his act or omission.

(4) Every one shall, until the contrary is proved, be presumed to be and to have been sane. 1953-54, c. 51, s. 16.

Section 16

Parties to Offences

21. (1) Every one is a party to an offence who
(a) actually commits it,
(b) does or omits to do anything for the purpose of aiding any person to commit it, or
(c) abets any person in committing it.

(2) Where two or more persons form an intention in common to carry out an unlawful purpose and to assist each other therein and any one of them, in carrying out the common purpose, commits an offence, each of them who knew or ought to have known that the commission of the offence would be a probable consequence of carrying out the common purpose is a party to that offence. 1953-54, c. 51, s. 21.

Section 21

Person Counselling Offence

22. (1) Where a person counsels another person to be a party to an offence and that other person is afterwards a party to that offence, the person who counselled is a party to that offence, notwithstanding that the offence was committed in a way different from that which was counselled.

Section 22

(2) Every one who counsels another person to be a party to an offence is a party to every offence that the other commits in consequence of the counselling that the person who counselled knew or ought to have known was likely to be committed in consequence of the counselling.
(3) For the purposes of this Act, "counsel" includes procure, solicit or incite, 1953-54, c. 51, s. 22; 1985, c. 19, s. 7(1).

Accessory after the Fact

Section 23

23. (1) An accessory after the fact to an offence is one who, knowing that a person has been a party to the offence, receives, comforts or assists him for the purpose of enabling him to escape.
(2) No married person whose spouse has been a party to an offence is an accessory after the fact to that offence by receiving, comforting or assisting the spouse for the purpose of enabling the spouse to escape. R.S., c. C-34, s. 23; 1974-75-76, c. 66, s. 7.
(3) Repealed, 1974-75-76, c. 66, s. 7.

23.1 For greater certainty, sections 21 to 23 apply in respect of an accused notwithstanding the fact that the person whom the accused aids or abets, counsels or procures or receives, comforts or assists cannot be convicted of the offence. 1986, c. 32, s. 44.

Offences Relating to Public or Peace Officer

Section 118

118. Every one who
(a) resists or wilfully obstructs a public officer or peace officer in the execution of his duty or any person lawfully acting in aid of such an officer,
(b) omits, without reasonable excuse, to assist a public officer or peace officer in the execution of his duty in arresting a person or in preserving the peace, after having reasonable notice that he is required to do so, or
(c) resists or wilfully obstructs any person in the lawful execution of a process against lands or goods or in making a lawful distress or seizure,
is guilty of
(d) an indictable offence and is liable to imprisonment for two years, or
(e) an offence punishable on summary conviction. R.S., c. C-34, s. 118; 1972, c. 13, s. 7.

Perjury

Section 120

120. (1) Subject to subsection (3), every one commits perjury who, with intent to mislead, makes before a person who is authorized by law to permit it to be made before him, a false statement under oath or solemn affirmation, by affidavit, solemn declaration or deposition or orally, knowing that the statement is false.

(2) Subsection (1) applies whether or not a statement referred to therein is made in a judicial proceeding.

(3) Subsection (1) does not apply to a statement referred to in that subsection that is made by a person who is not specially permitted, authorized or required by law to make that statement, 1985, c. 19, s. 17.

Punishment.
121. Every one who commits perjury is guilty of an indictable offence and is liable to imprisonment for a term not exceeding fourteen years, but if he commits perjury to procure the conviction of a person for an offence punishable by death, he is liable to a maximum term of imprisonment for life. 1985, c. 19, s. 17.

Section 121

Escape and Being at Large without Excuse
133. (1) Every one who
(a) escapes from lawful custody, or
(b) is, before the expiration of a term of imprisonment to which he was sentenced, at large in or out of Canada without lawful excuse, the proof of which lies upon him,
is guilty of an indictable offence and is liable to imprisonment for a term not exceeding two years or is guilty of an offence punishable on summary conviction.

Section 133

(2) Every one who,
(a) being at large on his undertaking or recognizance given to or entered into before a justice or judge, fails, without lawful excuse, the proof of which lies upon him, to attend court in accordance with the undertaking or recognizance, or
(b) having appeared before a court, justice or judge, fails, without lawful excuse, the proof of which lies upon him, to attend court as thereafter required by the court, justice or judge,
or to surrender himself in accordance with an order of the court, justice or judge, as the case may be, is guilty of an indictable offence and is liable to imprisonment for a term not exceeding two years or is guilty of an offence punishable on summary conviction. 1985, c. 19, s. 20(1).

(3) Every one who, being at large on his undertaking or recognizance given to or entered into before a justice or a judge and being bound to comply with a condition of that undertaking or recognizance directed by a justice or a judge, fails, without lawful excuse, the proof of which lies upon him, to comply with that condition, is guilty of

(a) an indictable offence and is liable to imprisonment for two years, or
(b) an offence punishable on summary conviction.

(4) Every one who is served with a summons and who fails, without lawful excuse, the proof of which lies upon him, to appear at a time and place stated therein, if any, for the purposes of the *Identification of Criminals Act* or to attend court in accordance therewith, is guilty of
(a) an indictable offence and is liable to imprisonment for two years, or
(b) an offence punishable on summary conviction.

(5) Every one who is named in an appearance notice or promise to appear, or in a recognizance entered into before an officer in charge, that has been confirmed by a justice under section 455.4 and who fails, without lawful excuse, the proof of which lies upon him, to appear at a time and place stated therein, if any, for the purposes of the *Identification of Criminals Act* or to attend court in accordance therewith, is guilty of
(a) an indictable offence and is liable to imprisonment for two years, or
(b) an offence punishable on summary conviction.

(6) For the purposes of subsection (5), it is not a lawful excuse that an appearance notice, promise to appear or recognizance states defectively the substance of the alleged offence.

(7) Repealed, 1985, c. 19, s. 20(2).

(8) For the purposes only of the *Identification of Criminals Act* a person charged with or convicted of an offence under this section punishable on summary conviction shall be deemed to be charged with or to have been convicted of an indictable offence.

(9) In any proceedings under subsection (2), (4) or (5), a certificate of the clerk of the court or a judge of the court before which the accused is alleged to have failed to attend or of the person in charge of the place at which it is alleged the accused failed to attend for the purposes of the *Identification of Criminals Act* stating that,
(a) in the case of proceedings under subsection (2), the accused gave or entered into an undertaking or recognizance before a justice or a judge and failed to attend court in accordance therewith,
(b) in the case of proceedings under subsection (4), a summons was issued to and served on the accused and the accused failed to attend court in accordance therewith or failed to appear at the time and place stated therein for the purposes of the *Identification of Criminals Act* as the case may be, and
(c) in the case of proceedings under subsection (5), the accused was named in an appearance notice, a promise to appear or a recognizance entered into before an officer in charge, that was confirmed by

a justice under section 455.4, and the accused failed to attend court in accordance therewith or failed to appear at the time and place stated therein for the purposes of the *Identification of Criminals Act* as the case may be, is evidence of the statements contained in the certificate without proof of the signature or the official character of the person appearing to have signed the certificate.

(10) An accused against whom a certificate described in subsection (9) is produced may, with leave of the court, require the attendance of the person making the certificate for the purposes of cross-examination.

(11) No certificate shall be received in evidence pursuant to subsection (9) unless the party intending to produce it has, before the trial, given to the accused reasonable notice of his intention together with a copy of the certificate. R.S., c. C-34, s. 133; R.S., c. 2(2nd Supp.), s. 4; 1974-75-76, c. 93, s. 7.

Assaulting a Peace Officer

246. (1) Every one commits an offence who   Section 246
- (a) assaults a public officer or peace officer engaged in the execution of his duty or a person acting in aid of such an officer;
- (b) assaults a person with intent to resist or prevent the lawful arrest or detention of himself or another person; or
- (c) assaults a person
    - (i) who is engaged in the lawful execution of a process against lands or goods or in making a lawful distress or seizure, or
    - (ii) with intent to rescue anything taken under lawful process, distress or seizure.

(2) Every one who commits an offence under subsection (1) is guilty of
- (a) an indictable offence and is liable to imprisonment for five years; or
- (b) an offence punishable on summary conviction. 1980-81-82, c. 125, s. 19.

Punishment for Theft

294. Except where otherwise provided by law, every   Section 294
one who commits theft
- (a) is guilty of an indictable offence and is liable to imprisonment for a term not exceeding ten years, where the property stolen is a testamentary instrument or where the value of what is stolen exceeds one thousand dollars;
- (b) is guilty
    - (i) of an indictable offence and is liable to imprisonment for two years, or
    - (ii) of an offence punishable on summary conviction,

where the value of what is stolen does not exceed one thousand dollars. R.S., c. C-34, s. 294; 1972, c. 13, s. 23; 1974-75-76, c. 93, s. 25; 1985, c. 19, s. 44.

Powers of Arrest — Definitions

448. In this Part

"accused" includes

    (a) a person to whom a peace officer has issued an appearance notice under section 451, and

    (b) a person arrested for a criminal offence;

"appearance notice" means a notice in Form 8.1 issued by a peace officer,

"judge" means

    (a) in the Province of Ontario, a judge of the superior court of criminal jurisdiction of the province or a judge of the District Court,

    (b) in the Province of Quebec, a judge of the superior court of criminal jurisdiction of the province or three judges of the sessions of the peace or of the provincial court,

    (c) in the Provinces of Nova Scotia and British Columbia, a judge of the superior court of criminal jurisdiction of the province or a judge of a county court,

    (d) in the Province of Newfoundland, a judge of the superior court of criminal jurisdiction of the Province or a judge of a district court,

    (d.1) in the Provinces of New Brunswick, Manitoba, Alberta and Saskatchewan, a judge of the superior court of criminal jurisdiction of the province,

    (e) in the Province of Prince Edward Island, the Yukon Territory and the Northwest Territories, a judge of the Supreme Court;

"officer in charge" means the officer for the time being in command of the police force responsible for the lock-up or other place to which an accused is taken after arrest or a peace officer designated by him for the purposes of this Part who is in charge of such place at the time an accused is taken to that place to be detained in custody;

"promise to appear" means a promise in Form 8.2 given to an officer in charge;

"recognizance", when used in relation to a recognizance entered into before an officer in charge, means a recognizance in Form 8.3, and when used in relation to a recognizance entered into before a justice or a judge, means a recognizance in Form 28;

"summons" means a summons in Form 6 issued by a justice or a judge;

"undertaking" means an undertaking in Form 9 given to a justice or a judge;

"warrant", when used in relation to a warrant for the arrest of a person, means a warrant in Form 7 and, when used in relation to a warrant for the committal of a person, means a warrant in Form 8. R.S., c. C-34, s. 448; R.S., c. 2(2nd Supp.), s. 5; 1972, c. 17, s. 2; 1974-75-76, c. 48, s. 25; 1984, c. 41, Schedule.

Arrest without Warrant and Release from Custody — Section 449

449. (1) Any one may arrest without warrant
 (a) a person whom he finds committing an indictable offence, or
 (b) a person who, on reasonable and probable grounds, he believes
  (i) has committed a criminal offence, and
  (ii) is escaping from and freshly pursued by persons who have lawful authority to arrest that person.
(2) Any one who is
 (a) the owner or a person in lawful possession of property, or
 (b) a person authorized by the owner or by a person in lawful possession of property,
may arrest without warrant a person whom he finds committing a criminal offence on or in relation to that property.
(3) Any one other than a peace officer who arrests a person without warrant shall forthwith deliver the person to a peace officer. R.S., c. C-34, s. 449; R.S., c. 2(2nd Supp.), s. 5.

450. (1) A peace officer may arrest without warrant — Section 450
 (a) a person who has committed an indictable offence or who, on reasonable and probable grounds, he believes has committed or is about to commit an indictable offence,
 (b) a person whom he finds committing a criminal offence, or
 (c) a person in respect of whom he has reasonable and probable grounds to believe that a warrant of arrest or committal, in any form set out in Part XXV in relation thereto, is in force within the territorial jurisdiction in which the person is found. 1985, c. 19, s. 76.
(2) A peace officer shall not arrest a person without warrant for
 (a) an indictable offence mentioned in section 483,
 (b) an offence for which the person may be prosecuted by indictment or for which he is punishable on summary conviction, or
 (c) an offence punishable on summary conviction, in any case where

(d) he has reasonable and probable grounds to believe that the public interest, having regard to all the circumstances including the need to
  (i) establish the identity of the person,
  (ii) secure or preserve evidence of or relating to the offence, or
  (iii) prevent the continuation or repetition of the offence or the commission of another offence,
may be satisfied without so arresting the person, and
(e) he has no reasonable grounds to believe that, if he does not so arrest the person, the person will fail to attend in court in order to be dealt with according to law.

(3) Notwithstanding subsection (2), a peace officer acting under subsection (1) is deemed to be acting lawfully and in the execution of his duty for the purposes of
(a) any proceedings under this or any other Act of Parliament, and
(b) any other proceedings, unless in any such proceedings it is alleged and established by the person making the allegation that the peace officer did not comply with the requirements of subsection (2). R.S., c. C-34, s. 450; R.S., c. 2(2nd Supp.), s. 5.

451. Where, by virtue of subsection 450(2), a peace officer does not arrest a person, he may issue an appearance notice to the person if the offence is
(a) an indictable offence mentioned in section 483,
(b) an offence for which the person may be prosecuted by indictment or for which he is punishable on summary conviction, or
(c) an offence punishable on summary conviction, R.S., c. C-34, s. 451; R.S., c. 2(2nd Supp.), s. 5.

452. (1) Where a peace officer arrests a person without warrant for
(a) an indictable offence mentioned in section 483,
(b) an offence for which the person may be prosecuted by indictment or for which he is punishable on summary conviction, or
(c) an offence punishable on summary conviction,
he shall, as soon as practicable,
(d) release the person from custody with the intention of compelling his appearance by way of summons, or

(e) issue an appearance notice to the person and thereupon release him, unless

(f) he has reasonable and probable grounds to believe that it is necessary in the public interest, having regard to all the circumstances including the need to

    (i) establish the identity of the person,

    (ii) secure or preserve evidence of or relating to the offence, or

    (iii) prevent the continuation or repetition of the offence or the commission of another offence,

that the person be detained in custody or that the matter of his release from custody be dealt with under another provision of this Part, or

(g) he has reasonable and probable grounds to believe that, if the person is released by him from custody, the person will fail to attend in court in order to be dealt with according to law.

(2) Subsection (1) does not apply in respect of a person who has been arrested without warrant by a peace officer for an offence described in subsection 454(2).

(3) A peace officer who has arrested a person without warrant for an offence described in subsection (1) and who does not release the person from custody as soon as practicable in the manner described in paragraph (d) or (e) of that subsection shall be deemed to be acting lawfully and in the execution of his duty for the purposes of

(a) any proceedings under this or any other Act of Parliament, and

(b) any other proceedings, unless in any such proceedings it is alleged and established by the person making the allegation that the peace officer did not comply with the requirements of subsection (1). R.S., c. C-34, s. 452; R.S., c. 2 (2nd Supp.), s. 5.

453. (1) Where a person who has been arrested without warrant by a peace officer is taken into custody, or where a person who has been arrested without warrant and delivered to a peace officer under subsection 449(3) is detained in custody under subsection 454(1) for

(a) an indictable offence mentioned in section 483,

(b) an offence for which the person may be prosecuted by indictment or for which he is punishable on summary conviction,

(c) an offence punishable on summary conviction, or

(d) any other offence that is punishable by imprisonment for five years or less,

and has not been taken before a justice or released from custody under any other provision of this Part, the officer in charge shall, as soon as practicable,

(e) release the person with the intention of compelling his appearance by way of summons,
(f) release the person upon his giving his promise to appear,
(g) release the person upon his entering into a recognizance before the officer in charge without sureties in such amount not exceeding five hundred dollars as the officer in charge directs, but without deposit of money or other valuable security, or
(h) if the person is not ordinarily resident in the province in which he is in custody or does not ordinarily reside within two hundred kilometres of the place in which he is in custody, release the person upon his entering into a recognizance before the officer in charge without sureties in such amount not exceeding five hundred dollars as the officer in charge directs and, if the officer in charge so directs, upon his depositing with the officer in charge such sum of money or other valuable security not exceeding in amount or value five hundred dollars, as the officer in charge directs,

unless
(i) he has reasonable and probable grounds to believe that it is necessary in the public interest, having regard to all the circumstances including the need to
(i) establish the identity of the person,
(ii) secure or preserve evidence of or relating to the offence, or
(iii) prevent the continuation or repetition of the offence or the commission of another offence,
that the person be detained in custody or that the matter of his release from custody be dealt with under another provision of this Part, or
(j) he has reasonable and probable grounds to believe that, if the person is released by him from custody, the person will fail to attend in court in order to be dealt with according to law. 1985, c. 19, s. 186.

(2) Subsection (1) does not apply in respect of a person who has been arrested without warrant by a peace officer for an offence described in subsection 454(2).

(3) An officer in charge who has the custody of a person taken into or detained in custody for an offence described in subsection (1) and who does not release the person from custody as soon as practicable in the manner described in paragraph (e), (f), (g) or (h) of that subsection shall be deemed to be acting lawfully and in the execution of his duty for the purposes of
(a) any proceedings under this or any other Act of Parliament, or

(b) any other proceedings, unless in any such proceedings it is alleged and established by the person making the allegation that the officer in charge did not comply with the requirements of subsection (1). R.S., c. C-34, s. 453; R.S., c. 2 (2nd Supp.), s. 5.

Arrest with a Warrant

453.1 Where a person who has been arrested with a warrant by a peace officer is taken into custody for

(a) an indictable offence mentioned in section 483,
(b) an offence for which the person may be prosecuted by indictment or for which he is punishable on summary conviction,
(c) an offence punishable on summary conviction, or
(d) any other offence that is punishable by imprisonment for five years or less,

the officer in charge may, if the warrant has been endorsed by a justice under subsection 455.3(6),

(e) release the person upon his giving his promise to appear,
(f) release the person upon his entering into a recognizance before the officer in charge without sureties in such amount not exceeding five hundred dollars as the officer in charge directs, but without deposit of money or other valuable security, or
(g) if the person is not ordinarily resident in the province in which he is in custody or does not ordinarily reside within two hundred kilometres of the place in which he is in custody, release the person upon his entering into a recognizance before the officer in charge without sureties in such amount not exceeding five hundred dollars as the officer in charge directs and, if the officer in charge so directs, upon his depositing with the officer in charge such sum of money or other valuable security not exceeding in amount or value five hundred dollars, as the officer in charge directs. 1985, c. 19, s. 186.

Section 453.1

453.2 Where a person has, pursuant to paragraph 453(1)(h) or paragraph 453.1(g), deposited any sum of money or other valuable security with the officer in charge, the officer in charge shall, forthwith after the deposit thereof, cause the money or valuable security to be delivered to a justice for deposit with the justice. R.S., c. 2 (2nd Supp.), s. 5.

Section 453.2

Appearance of Accused before Justice

454. (1) A peace officer who arrests a person with or without warrant or to whom a person is delivered under subsection 449(3) shall cause the person to be detained in custody and, in accordance with the following provisions,

Section 454

to be taken before a justice to be dealt with according to law, namely:
- (a) where a justice is available within a period of twenty-four hours after the person has been arrested by or delivered to the peace officer, the person shall be taken before a justice without unreasonable delay and in any event within that period, and
- (b) where a justice is not available within a period of twenty-four hours after the person has been arrested by or delivered to the peace officer, the person shall be taken before a justice as soon as possible,

unless, at any time before the expiration of the time prescribed in paragraph (a) or (b) for taking the person before a justice,
- (c) the peace officer or officer in charge releases the person under any other provision of this Part, or
- (d) the peace officer or officer in charge is satisfied that the person should be released from custody, whether unconditionally under subsection (3) or otherwise conditionally or unconditionally, and so releases him.

(1.1) Where a peace officer or an officer in charge is satisfied that a person described in subsection (1) should be released from custody conditionally, he may, unless the person is detained in custody for an offence mentioned in section 457.7, release that person in accordance with paragraphs 453(1)(f) to (h).

(2) Where a person has been arrested without warrant for an indictable offence alleged to have been committed in Canada outside the province in which he was arrested, he shall, within the time prescribed in paragraphs (1)(a) and (b), be taken before a justice within whose jurisdiction he was arrested and the justice,
- (a) if he is not satisfied that there are reasonable and probable grounds to believe that the person arrested is the person alleged to have committed the offence, shall release him; or
- (b) if he is satisfied that there are reasonable and probable grounds to believe that the person arrested is the person alleged to have committed the offence, may remand him to the custody of a peace officer to await execution of a warrant for his arrest in accordance with section 461, but if no warrant for his arrest is so executed within a period of six days after the time he is remanded to such custody, the person in whose custody he then is shall release him.

(2.1) Notwithstanding paragraph (2)(b), a justice may, with the consent of the prosecutor, order that the person

referred to in subsection (2), pending the execution of a warrant for his arrest, be released
   (a) unconditionally, or
   (b) on any of the following terms to which the prosecutor consents, namely,
      (i) giving an undertaking, or
      (ii) entering into a recognizance described in any of paragraphs 457(2)(a) to (d)
with such conditions described in subsection 457(4) as the justice considers desirable and to which the prosecutor consents. 1985, c. 19, s. 78.

(3) A peace officer or officer in charge having the custody of a person who has been arrested without warrant as a person about to commit an indictable offence shall release that person unconditionally as soon as practicable after he is satisfied that the continued detention of that person in custody is no longer necessary in order to prevent the commission by him of an indictable offence.

(4) Notwithstanding subsection (3), a peace officer or officer in charge having the custody of a person referred to in that subsection who does not release the person before the expiration of the time prescribed in paragraph (1)(a) or (b) for taking the person before the justice, shall be deemed to be acting lawfully and in the execution of his duty for the purposes of
   (a) any proceedings under this or any other Act of Parliament, or
   (b) any other proceedings, unless in such proceedings it is alleged and established by the person making the allegation that the peace officer or officer in charge did not comply with the requirements of subsection (3). R.S., c. C-34, s. 454; R.S., c. 2 (2nd Supp.), s. 5; 1974-75-76, c. 93, s. 46.

457. (1) Subject to this section, where an accused who is charged with an offence other than an offence listed in section 427 is taken before a justice the justice shall, unless a plea of guilty by the accused is accepted, order, in respect of that offence, that the accused be released upon his giving an undertaking without conditions, unless the prosecutor, having been given a reasonable opportunity to do so, shows cause, in respect of that offence, why the detention of the accused in custody is justified or why an order under any other provision of this section should be made and where the justice makes an order under any other provision of this section, the order shall refer only to the particular offence for which the accused was taken before the justice. 1985, c. 19, s. 84(1).

(2) Where the justice does not make an order under subsection (1), he shall, unless the prosecutor shows cause

why the detention of the accused is justified, order that the accused be released
- (a) upon his giving an undertaking with such conditions as the justice directs,
- (b) upon his entering into a recognizance before the justice, without sureties, in such amount and with such conditions, if any, as the justice directs but without deposit of money or other valuable security,
- (c) upon his entering into a recognizance before the justice with sureties in such amount and with such conditions, if any, as the justice directs but without deposit of money or other valuable security,
- (c.1) with the consent of the prosecutor, upon his entering into a recognizance before the justice, without sureties, in such amount and with such conditions, if any, as the justice directs and upon his depositing with the justice such sum of money or other valuable security as the justice directs, or
- (d) if the accused is not ordinarily resident in the province in which he is in custody or does not ordinarily reside within two hundred kilometres of the place in which he is in custody, upon his entering into a recognizance before the justice with or without sureties in such amount and with such conditions, if any, as the justice directs, and upon his depositing with the justice such sum of money or other valuable security as the justice directs. 1985, c. 19, Schedule IV, Item 7.

(2.1) Where, pursuant to subsection (2) or any other provision of this Act, a justice, judge or court orders that an accused be released upon his entering into a recognizance with sureties, the justice, judge or court may, in the order, name particular persons as sureties. 1985, c. 19, ss. 84(2), 186.

(3) The justice shall not make an order under any of paragraphs (2)(b) to (d) unless the prosecution shows cause why an order under the immediately preceding paragraph should not be made.

(4) The justice may direct as conditions under subsection (2) that the accused shall do any one or more of the following things as specified in the order, namely:
- (a) report at times to be stated in the order to a peace officer or other person designated in the order;
- (b) remain within a territorial jurisdiction specified in the order;
- (c) notify the peace officer or other person designated under paragraph (a) of any change in his address or his employment or occupation;
- (d) abstain from communicating with any witness or other person expressly named in the order except in accordance with such conditions specified in the order as the justice deems necessary;

(e) where the accused is the holder of a passport, deposit his passport as specified in the order; and
(f) comply with such other reasonable conditions specified in the order as the justice considers desirable.

(5) Where the prosecutor shows cause why the detention of the accused in custody is justified, the justice shall order that the accused be detained in custody until he is dealt with according to law and shall include in the record a statement of his reasons for making the order.

(5.1) Notwithstanding any provision of this section, where an accused is charged
(a) with an indictable offence, other than an offence listed in section 427, that is alleged to have been committed while he was at large after being released in respect of another indictable offence pursuant to the provisions of this Part or section 608 or 608.1,
(b) with an indictable offence, other than an offence listed in section 427 and is not ordinarily resident in Canada,
(c) with an offence under any of subsections 133(2) to (5) that is alleged to have been committed while he was at large after being released in respect of another offence pursuant to the provisions of this Part or section 608, 608.1 or 752, or
(d) with having committed an offence under section 4 or 5 of the *Narcotic Control Act* or the offence of conspiring to commit an offence under section 4 or 5 of the *Narcotic Control Act*

the justice shall order that the accused be detained in custody until he is dealt with according to law, unless the accused, having been given a reasonable opportunity to do so, shows cause why his detention in custody is not justified, but where the justice orders that the accused be released, he shall include in the record a statement of his reasons for making the order. 1985, c. 19, s. 84(3).

(5.2) Where an accused to whom paragraph (5.1)(a), (c) or (d) applies shows cause why his detention in custody is not justified, the justice shall order that he be released upon his giving an undertaking or entering into a recognizance described in any of paragraphs (2)(a) to (d) with such conditions described in subsection (4) or, where the accused was at large upon an undertaking or recognizance with conditions, such additional conditions described in subsection (4), as the justice considers desirable, unless the accused, having been given a reasonable opportunity to do so, shows cause why such conditions or additional conditions should not be imposed.

(5.3) Where an accused to whom paragraph (5.1)(b) applies shows cause why his detention in custody is not justified, the justice shall order that he be released upon his giving an undertaking or entering into a recognizance described in any of paragraphs (2)(a) to (d) with such conditions, described in subsection (4), as the justice considers desirable.

(6) For the purposes of subsections (5) and (5.1), it is sufficient if a record is made of the reasons in accordance with the provisions of Part XV relating to the taking of evidence at preliminary inquiries.

(7) For the purposes of this section, the detention of an accused in custody is justified only on either of the following grounds, namely:
    (a) on the primary ground that his detention is necessary to ensure his attendance in court in order to be dealt with according to law; and
    (b) on the secondary ground (the applicability of which shall be determined only in the event that and after it is determined that his detention is not justified on the primary ground referred to in paragraph (a)) that his detention is necessary in the public interest or for the protection or safety of the public, having regard to all the circumstances including any substantial likelihood that the accused will, if he is released from custody, commit a criminal offence or an interference with the administration of justice.

(8) Where an accused who is charged with an offence listed in section 427 is taken before a justice, the justice shall order that the accused be detained in custody until he is dealt with according to law and shall issue a warrant in Form 8 for the committal of the accused. R.S., c. C-34, s. 457; R.S., c. 2 (2nd Supp.), s. 5; 1974-75-76, c. 93, s. 47; 1985, c. 19, s. 84(4).

Section 457.1

457.1 A justice may, before or at any time during the course of any proceedings under section 457, upon application by the prosecutor or the accused, adjourn the proceedings and remand the accused to custody in prison by warrant in Form 14, but no such adjournment shall be for more than three clear days except with the consent of the accused. R.S., c. 2 (2nd Supp.), s. 5.

Section 457.2

457.2 (1) Where the prosecutor or the accused intends to show cause under section 457, he shall so state to the justice and the justice may, and shall upon application by the accused, before or at any time during the course of the proceedings under that section, make an order directing that the evidence taken, the information given or the representations made and the reasons, if any, given or to be given by the justice shall not be published in any newspaper or broadcast before such time as

(a) if a preliminary inquiry is held, the accused in respect of whom the proceedings are held is discharged, or
(b) if the accused in respect of whom the proceedings are held is tried or ordered to stand trial, the trial is ended. 1985, c. 19, s. 101(2).

(2) Every one who fails without lawful excuse, the proof of which lies upon him, to comply with an order made under subsection (1) is guilty of an offence punishable on summary conviction.

(3) In this section, "newspaper" has the same meaning as it has in sections 262 to 281 by virtue of section 261. R.S., c. 2 (2nd Supp.), s. 5; 1974-75-76, c. 93, s. 48.

457.3 (1) In any proceedings under section 457,   Section 457.3
(a) the justice may, subject to paragraph (b), make such inquiries, on oath or otherwise, of and concerning the accused as he considers desirable;
(b) the accused shall not be examined or cross-examined by the justice or any other person as to the offence with which he is charged, and no inquiry shall be made of him as to that offence;
(c) the prosecutor may, in addition to any other relevant evidence, lead evidence
   (i) to prove that the accused has previously been convicted of a criminal offence,
   (ii) to prove that the accused has been charged with and is awaiting trial for another criminal offence,
   (iii) to prove that the accused has previously committed an offence under section 133, or
   (iv) to show the circumstances of the alleged offence, particularly as they relate to the probability of conviction of the accused;
(d) the justice may take into consideration any relevant matters agreed upon by the prosecutor and the accused or his counsel;
(d.1) the justice may receive evidence obtained as a result of an interception of a private communication under and within the meaning of Part IV.1, in writing, orally or in the form of a recording and, for the purposes of this section, subsection 178.16(4) does not apply to such evidence; and
(e) the justice may receive and base his decision upon evidence considered credible or trustworthy by him in the circumstances of each case. 1985, c. 19, s. 85(1).

(2) Where, before or at any time during the course of any proceedings under section 457, the accused pleads guilty and his plea is accepted, the justice may make any order provided for in this Part for the release of the accused until

he is sentenced. R.S., c. 2 (2nd Supp.), s. 5; 1974-75-76, c. 93, s. 49; 1985, c. 19, s. 85(2).

Section 457.4

457.4 (1) Where a justice makes an order under subsection 457(1), (2), (5.2) or (5.3),
  (a) if the accused thereupon complies with the order, the justice shall direct that he be released
    (i) forthwith, if the accused is not required to be detained in custody in respect of any other matter, or
    (ii) as soon thereafter as the accused is no longer required to be detained in custody in respect of any other matter; and
  (b) if the accused does not thereupon comply with the order, the justice who made the order or another justice having jurisdiction shall issue a warrant for the committal of the accused and may endorse thereon an authorization to the person having the custody of the accused to release the accused when the accused complies with the order
    (i) forthwith after the compliance, if the accused is not required to be detained in custody in respect of any other matter, or
    (ii) as soon thereafter as he is no longer required to be detained in custody in respect of any other matter

and if the justice so endorses the warrant, he shall attach it to a copy of the order.

(2) Where the accused complies with an order referred to in paragraph (1)(b), and he is not required to be detained in custody in respect of any other matter, the justice who made the order or another justice having jurisdiction shall, unless the accused has been or will be released pursuant to an authorization referred to in that paragraph, issue an order for discharge in Form 35. 1985, c. 19, s. 86.

(3) Where the justice makes an order under subsection 457(5) or (5.1) for the detention of the accused, he shall issue a warrant for the committal of the accused. R.S., c. 2 (2nd Supp.), s. 5; 1974-75-76, c. 93, s. 50.

Section 457.8

457.8 (1) Where an accused, in respect of an offence with which he is charged, has not been taken into custody or has been released from custody under or by virtue of any provision of this Part, the appearance notice, promise to appear, summons, undertaking or recognizance issued to, given or entered into by him continues in force, subject to its terms, and applies in respect of any new information charging the same offence or an included offence that was received after the appearance notice, promise to appear, summons, undertaking or recognizance was issued, given or entered into,

(a) where the accused was released from custody pursuant to an order of a judge made under subsection 457.7(2), until his trial is completed, or
(b) in any other case,
   (i) until his trial is completed, and
   (ii) where the accused is, at his trial, determined to be guilty of the offence, until a sentence within the meaning of section 601 is imposed on the accused unless, at the time he is determined to be guilty, the court, judge or justice orders that the accused be taken into custody pending such sentence.

(1.1) Where an accused, in respect of an offence with which he is charged, has not been taken into custody or is being detained or has been released from custody under or by virtue of any provision of this Part and after the order for interim release or detention has been made, or the appearance notice, promise to appear, summons, undertaking or recognizance has been issued, given or entered into, a new information charging the same offence or an included offence, is received, section 455.3 or 455.4, as the case may be, does not apply in respect of the new information and the order for interim release or detention of the accused and the appearance notice, promise to appear, summons, undertaking or recognizance, if any, applies in respect of the new information. 1985, c. 19, s. 90(1)-(3).

(2) Notwithstanding subsections (1) and (1.1),
(a) the court, judge or justice before whom an accused is being tried, at any time,
(b) the justice, on completion of the preliminary inquiry in relation to an offence for which an accused is ordered to stand trial, other than an offence listed in section 427, or
(c) with the consent of the prosecutor and the accused or, where the accused or the prosecutor applies to vacate an order that would otherwise apply pursuant to subsection (1.1), without such consent, at any time
   (i) where the accused is charged with an offence other than an offence listed in section 427, the justice by whom an order was made under this Part or any other justice,
   (ii) where the accused is charged with an offence listed in section 427, a judge of or a judge presiding in a superior court of criminal jurisdiction for the province, or
   (iii) the court, judge or justice before whom an accused is to be tried, may, on cause being shown, vacate any order previously made

under this Part for the interim release or detention of the accused and make any other order provided for in this Part for the detention or release of the accused until his trial is completed that the court, judge or justice considers to be warranted. R.S., c. 2 (2nd Supp.), s. 5; 1974-75-76, c. 93, s. 54; 1985, c. 19, s. 90(4).

(3) The provisions of sections 457.2, 457.3 and 457.4 apply, with such modifications as the circumstances require, in respect of any proceedings under subsection (2), except that subsection 457.3(2) does not apply in respect of an accused who is charged with an offence listed in section 427. 1985, c. 19, s. 90(4).

Proof of Previous Conviction

594. (1) In any proceedings,
 (a) a certificate setting out with reasonable particularity the conviction, discharge under section 662.1 or the conviction and sentence in Canada of an offender signed by
  (i) the person who made the conviction or order for the discharge,
  (ii) the clerk of the court in which the conviction or order for the discharge was made, or
  (iii) a fingerprint examiner,
 is, on proof that the accused or defendant is the offender referred to in the certificate, evidence that the accused or defendant was so convicted, so discharged or so convicted and sentenced without proof of the signature or the official character of the person appearing to have signed the certificate;
 (b) evidence that the fingerprints of the accused or defendant are the same as the fingerprints of the offender whose fingerprints are reproduced in or attached to a certificate issued under subparagraph (a)(iii) is, in the absence of evidence to the contrary, proof that the accused or defendant is the offender referred to in that certificate;
 (c) a certificate of a fingerprint examiner stating that he has compared the fingerprints reproduced in or attached to that certificate with the fingerprints reproduced in or attached to a certificate issued under sub-paragraph (a)(iii) and that they are those of the same person is evidence of the statements contained in the certificate without proof of the signature or the official character of the person appearing to have signed the certificate; and

(d) a certificate under subparagraph (a)(iii) may be in Form 42, and a certificate under paragraph (c) may be in Form 43. 1985, c. 19, s. 134(1).

(2) In any proceedings, a copy of the summary conviction or discharge under section 662.1 in Canada of an offender, signed by the person who made the conviction or order for the discharge or by the clerk of the court in which the conviction or order for the discharge was made, is, on proof that the accused or defendant is the offender referred to in the copy of the summary conviction, evidence of the conviction or discharge under section 662.1 of the accused or defendant, without proof of the signature or the official character of the person appearing to have signed it. 1985, c. 19, s. 134(2).

(2.1) In any summary conviction proceedings, where the name of a defendant is similar to the name of an offender referred to in a certificate made under subparagraph (1)(a)(i) or (ii) in respect of a summary conviction or referred to in a copy of a summary conviction mentioned in subsection (2), that similarity of name is, in the absence of evidence to the contrary, evidence that the defendant is the offender referred to in the certificate or the copy of the summary conviction. 1985, c. 19, s. 134(2).

(3) An accused against whom a certificate issued under subparagraph (1)(a)(iii) or paragraph (1)(c) is produced may, with leave of the court, require the attendance of the person who signed the certificate for the purposes of cross-examination.

(3.1) No certificate issued under subparagraph (1)(a)(iii) or paragraph (1)(c) shall be received in evidence unless the party intending to produce it has given to the accused reasonable notice of his intention together with a copy of the certificate.

(4) In this section "fingerprint examiner" means a person designated as such for the purposes of this section by the Solicitor General of Canada. R.S., c. C-34, s. 594; 1972, c. 13, s. 51.

Warrant when Witness Does Not Attend

633. (1) Where a person who has been served with a subpoena to give evidence in a proceeding does not attend or remain in attendance, the court, judge, justice or provincial court judge before whom that person was required to attend may, if it is established

(a) that the subpoena has been served in accordance with this Part, and

(b) that the person is likely to give material evidence, issue or cause to be issued a warrant in Form 12 for the arrest of that person. 1985, c. 19, s. 206.

(2) Where a person who has been bound by a recogni-

zance to attend to give evidence in any proceeding does not attend or does not remain in attendance, the court, judge, justice or provincial court judge before whom that person was bound to attend may issue or cause to be issued a warrant in Form 12 for the arrest of that person. 1985, c. 19, s. 206.

(3) A warrant that is issued by a justice or provincial court judge pursuant to subsection (1) or (2) may be executed anywhere in Canada. 1953-54, c. 51, s. 610; 1985, c. 19, s. 206.

Render of Accused by Sureties

Section 700

700. (1) A surety for a person who is bound by recognizance to appear may, by an application in writing to a court, justice or provincial court judge apply to be relieved of his obligation under the recognizance, and the court, justice or provincial court judge shall thereupon issue an order in writing for committal of that person to the prison nearest to the place where he was, under the recognizance, bound to appear. 1985, c. 19, s. 206.

(2) An order under subsection (1) shall be given to the surety and upon receipt thereof he or any peace officer may arrest the person named in the order and deliver him with the order to the keeper of the prison named herein, and the keeper shall receive and imprison him until he is discharged according to law. 1985, c. 19, s. 206.

(3) Where a judge, justice or provincial court judge who issues an order under subsection (1) receives from the sheriff a certificate that the person named in the order has been committed to prison pursuant to subsection (2), he shall order an entry of the committal to be endorsed on the recognizance. 1985, c. 19, s. 206.

(4) An endorsement under subsection (3) vacates the recognizance and discharges the sureties. 1953-54, c. 51, s. 672.

Application of Judicial Interim Release Provisions

Section 703

703. Where a surety for a person has rendered him into custody and that person has been committed to prison, the provisions of Parts XIV, XVIII and XXIV relating to judicial interim release apply, *mutatis mutandis* in respect of him and he shall forthwith be taken before a justice or judge as an accused charged with an offence or as an appellant, as the case may be, for the purposes of those provisions. R.S., c. C-34, s. 703; R.S., c. 2(2nd Supp.), s. 14.

General Penalty

722. (1) Except where otherwise provided by law, every one who is convicted of an offence punishable on summary conviction is liable to a fine of not more than two thousand dollars or to imprisonment for six months or to both. 1985, c. 19, s. 170(1).

(2) Where the imposition of a fine or the making of an order for the payment of money is authorized by law, but the law does not provide that imprisonment may be imposed in default of payment of the fine or compliance with the order, the court may order that in default of payment of the fine or compliance with the order, as the case may be, the defendant shall be imprisoned for a period of not more than six months. 1953-54, c. 51, s. 694; 1959, c. 41, s. 31.

(3) to (11) Repealed, 1985, c. 19, s. 170(2).

Appendix C — Forms

(1) UNDERTAKING GIVEN TO A JUSTICE OR A JUDGE (1) Undertaking
(Sections 457, 457.5, 457.6, 457.7, 458, 459, (Judge)
608 and 608.1)
Canada,

    Province of ....,
    (*territorial division*).

I, A.B., of ...., (*occupation*) understand that I have been charged that (*set out briefly the offence in respect of which accused is charged*).

In order that I may be released from custody, I undertake to attend court on .... day, the .... day of .... A.D. ...., and to attend thereafter as required by the court in order to be dealt with according to law *or* (*where date and place of appearance before court are not known at the time undertaking is given*) to attend at the time and place fixed by the court and thereafter as required by the court in order to be dealt with according to law.

    (and where applicable)

I also undertake to (*insert any conditions that are directed*)
    (a) report at (*state times*) to (*name of peace officer or other person designated*),
    (b) remain within (*designated territorial jurisdiction*),
    (c) notify (*name of peace officer or other person designated*) of any change in my address, employment or occupation,
    (d) abstain from communication with (*name of witness or other person*) except in accordance with the following conditions: (*as the justice or judge specifies*),
    (e) deposit my passport (*as the justice or judge directs*), and
    (f) (*any other reasonable conditions*).

I understand that failure without lawful excuse to attend court in accordance with this undertaking is an offence under subsection 133(2) of the *Criminal Code*.

Subsections 133(2) and (3) of the *Criminal Code* state as follows:

    "(2) Every one who,
    (a) being at large on his undertaking or recognizance given to or entered into before a justice or judge, fails, without lawful excuse, the proof of which

lies upon him, to attend court in accordance with the undertaking or recognizance, or

(b) having appeared before a court, justice or judge, fails, without lawful excuse, the proof of which lies upon him, to attend court as thereafter required by the court, justice or judge,

or to surrender himself in accordance with an order of the court, justice or judge, as the case may be, is guilty of an indictable offence and is liable to imprisonment for a term not exceeding two years or is guilty of an offence punishable on summary conviction.

(3) Every one who, being at large on his undertaking or recognizance given to or entered into before a justice or a judge and being bound to comply with a condition of that undertaking or recognizance directed by a justice or a judge, fails, without lawful excuse, the proof of which lies upon him, to comply with that condition, is guilty of

(a) an indictable offence and is liable to imprisonment for two years, or

(b) an offence punishable on summary conviction.''

Dated this .... day of .... A.D. ...., at ....

....
(*Signature of accused*)

R.S., c. C-34, s. 774 (Form 9); R.S., c. 2 (2nd Supp.), s. 23(2); 1985, c. 19, s. 184(6).

(2) Recognizance (Judge)

(2) **RECOGNIZANCE**

Canada,

Province of ....,
(*territorial division*).

Be it remembered that on this day the persons named in the following schedule personally came before me and severally acknowledged themselves to owe to Her Majesty the Queen the several amounts set opposite their respective names, namely,

Name	Address	Occupation	Amount
A.B.			
C.D.			
E.F.			

to be made and levied of their several goods and chattels, lands and tenements, respectively, to the use of Her Majesty the Queen, if the said A.B. fails in any of the conditions hereunder written.

Taken and acknowledged before me on the ...... day of ...... A.D. ...., at ....

....
Judge, Clerk of the Court,
Provincial Court Judge *or* Justice

1. Whereas the said ...., hereinafter called the accused, has been charged that (*set out the offence in respect of which the accused has been charged*);

Now, therefore, the condition of this recognizance is that if the accused attends court on .... day, the ...... day of ...... A.D. ...., at .... o'clock in the .... noon and attends thereafter as required by the court in order to be dealt with according to law *or* (*where date and place of appearance before court are not known at the time recognizance is entered into*) if the accused attends at the time and place fixed by the court and attends thereafter as required by the court in order to be dealt with according to law [457; 457.5; 457.6; 457.7; 457.8; 458; 459; 608.1];

And further, if the accused (*insert in Schedule of Conditions any additional conditions that are directed*),

the said recognizance is void, otherwise it stands in full force and effect.

2. Whereas the said ...., hereinafter called the appellant, is an appellant against his conviction (*or* against his sentence) in respect of the following charge (*set out the offence for which the appellant was convicted*) [608; 608.1]:

Now, therefore, the condition of this recognizance is that if the appellant attends as required by the court in order to be dealt with according to law;

And further, if the appellant (*insert in Schedule of Conditions any additional conditions that are directed*),

the said recognizance is void, otherwise it stands in full force and effect.

3. Whereas the said ...., hereinafter called the appellant, is an appellant against his conviction (*or against his sentence or* against an order *or* by way of stated case) in respect of the following matter (*set out offence, subject matter of order or question of law*) [752; 763; 764; 766]:

Now, therefore, the condition of this recognizance is that if the appellant appears personally at the sittings of the appeal court at which the appeal is to be heard;

And further, if the appellant (*insert in Schedule of Conditions any additional conditions that are directed*), the said recognizance is void, otherwise it stands in full force and effect.

4. Whereas the said ...., hereinafter called the appellant, is an appellant against an order of dismissal (*or* against sentence) in respect of the following charge (*set out the name of the defendant and the offence, subject matter of order or question of law*) [752.1; 763; 764; 766]:

Now therefore, the condition of this recognizance is that if the appellant appears personally or by counsel at the sittings of the appeal court at which the appeal is to be heard the said recognizance is void, otherwise it stands in full force and effect.

5. Whereas the said ...., hereinafter called the accused, was ordered to stand trial on a charge that (*set out the offence in respect of which the accused has been charged*);

And whereas A.B. appeared as witness on the preliminary inquiry into the said charge [477; 634; 635];

Now, therefore, the condition of this recognizance is that if the said A.B. appears at the time and place fixed for the trial of the accused to give evidence upon the indictment that is found against the accused, the said recognizance is void, otherwise it stands in full force and effect.

6. The condition of the above written recognizance is that if A.B. keeps the peace and is of good behaviour for the term of .... commencing on ...., the said recognizance is void, otherwise it stands in full force and effect [745].

Schedule of Conditions

(a) reports at (*state times*) to (*name of peace officer or other person designated*),
(b) remains within (*designated territorial jurisdiction*),
(c) notifies (*name of peace officer or other person designated*) of any change in his address, employment or occupation,
(d) abstains from communicating with (*name of witness or other person*) except in accordance with the following conditions: (*as the justice or judge specifies*),
(e) deposits his passport (*as the justice or judge directs*), and
(f) (*any other reasonable conditions*).

Note: Section 697 and subsections 698(1), (2) and (3) of the *Criminal Code* state as follows:

697. Where a person is bound by recognizance to appear before a court, justice or provincial court judge for any purpose and the session or sittings of that court or the proceedings are adjourned or an order is made changing the place of trial, that person and his sureties continue to be bound by the recognizance in like manner as if it had been entered into with relation to the resumed proceedings or the trial at the time and place at which the proceedings are ordered to be resumed or the trial is ordered to be held.

698. (1) Where an accused is bound by recognizance to appear for trial, his arraignment or conviction does not discharge the recognizance, but it continues to bind him and his sureties, if any, for his appearance until he is discharged or sentenced, as the case may be.

(2) Notwithstanding subsection (1), the court, justice or provincial court judge may commit an accused to prison or may require him to furnish new or additional sureties for this appearance until he is discharged or sentenced, as the case may be.

(3) The sureties of an accused who is bound by recognizance to appear for trial are discharged if he is committed to prison pursuant to subsection (2). R.S., c C-34, s. 773 (Form 28); R.S., c. 2 (2nd Supp.), s. 23(8); 1985, c. 19, ss. 101(2), 184(13), 206.

(3) SUMMONS TO A PERSON CHARGED WITH AN OFFENCE
(Sections 455.3, 455.4, 455.5 and 456.1)

(3) Summons (Police) including requirement to attend for prints.

Canada,
    Province of ....,
    (territorial division).
To A.B., of .... *(occupation)*:

Whereas you have this day been charged before me that *(set out briefly the offence in respect of which the accused is charged)*;

This is therefore to command you, in Her Majesty's name:

1. to attend court on ...., the .... day of ...... A.D. ...., at .... o'clock in the ..... noon, at .... or before any justice for the said *(territorial division)* who is there, and to attend thereafter as required by the court, in order to be dealt with according to law, and

2. to appear on ...., the .... day of ...... A.D. ...., at .... o'clock in the ..... noon, at ...., for the purpose of the *Identification of Criminals Act.* *(Ignore, if not filled in).*

You are warned that failure without lawful excuse to attend court in accordance with this summons is an offence under subsection 133(4) of the *Criminal Code.*

Subsection 133(4) of the *Criminal Code* states as follows:

"(4) Every one who is served with a summons and who fails, without lawful excuse, the proof of which lies upon him, to appear at a time and place stated therein, if any, for the purposes of the *Identification of Criminals Act* or to attend court in accordance therewith, is guilty of accordance therewith, is guilty of

(a) an indictable offence and is liable to imprisonment for two years, or
(b) an offence punishable on summary conviction.''
Section 455.6 of the *Criminal Code* states as follows:

"**455.** Where an accused who is required by a summons to appear at a time and place stated therein for the purposes of the *Identification of Criminals Act* does not appear at that time and place, a justice may issue a warrant for the arrest of the accused for the offence with which he is charged.''

Dated this .... day of .... A.D. ...., at ....

....
A Justice of the Peace in and for .... *or* Judge

R.S., c. C-34, s. 773 (Form 6); R.S., c. 2 (2nd Supp.), s. 23(2); 1985, c. 19, s. 184(4).

(4) Appearance Notice (Police) and requirement to attend for prints and photos

(4) APPEARANCE NOTICE ISSUED BY A PEACE OFFICER TO A PERSON NOT YET CHARGED WITH AN OFFENCE
(Sections 451 and 452)

Canada,
    Province of ....,
    (*territorial division*).
    To A.B., of .... (*occupation*):
You are alleged to have committed (*set out substance of offence*).

1. You are required to attend court on .... day, the .... day of ...... A.D. ...., at .... o'clock in the ..... noon, in courtroom No. ...., at .... court, in the municipality of ...., and to attend thereafter as required by the court, in order to be dealt with according to law.

2. You are also required to appear on .... day, the .... day of ...... A.D. ...., at .... o'clock in the ..... noon, at (*police station*), (*address*), for the purpose of the *Identification of Criminals Act*. (*Ignore, if not filled in*).

You are warned that failure to attend court in accordance with this summons is an offence under subsection 133(5) of the *Criminal Code*.

Subsection 133(5) and (6) of the *Criminal Code* states as follows:

"(5) Every one who is named in an appearance notice or promise to appear, or in a recognizance entered into before an officer in charge, that has been confirmed by a justice under section 455.4 and who fails, without lawful excuse, the proof of which lies upon him, to attend court in accordance therewith, is guilty of

(a) an indictable offence and is liable to imprisonment for two years, or
(b) an offence punishable on summary conviction.

(6) For the purposes of subsection (5), it is not a lawful excuse that an appearance notice, promise to appear or recognizance states defectively the substance of the alleged offence."

Section 453.4 of the *Criminal Code* states as follows:

"**453.4** Where an accused who is required by an appearance notice or promise to appear or by a recognizance entered into before an officer in charge to appear at a time and place stated therein for the purposes of the *Identification of Criminals Act* does not appear at that time and place, a justice may, where the appearance notice, promise to appear or recognizance has been confirmed by a justice under section 455.4 issue a warrant for the arrest of the accused for the offence with which he is charged."

Issued at .... a.m./p.m. this .... day of .... A.D. ...., at ....

....
(*Signature of peace officer*)
....
(*Signature of accused*)

R.S., c. 2 (2nd Supp.) s. 23(2); 1985, c. 19, s. 184(5).

(5) **PROMISE TO APPEAR** (Sections 453 and 453.1)

Canada,
        Province of ....,
        (*territorial division*).

I, A.B., of .... (*occupation*), understand that it is alleged that I have committed (*set out substance of offence*).

In order that I may be released from custody,

1. I promise to attend court on .... day, the .... day of ...... A.D. ...., at .... o'clock in the ..... noon, in courtroom No. ...., at court in the municipality of ...., and to attend thereafter as required by the court, in order to be dealt with according to law.

2. I also promise to appear on .... day, the .... day of ...... A.D. ...., at .... o'clock in the ..... noon, at (*police station*), (*address*), for the purpose of the *Identification of Criminals Act*. (*Ignore, if not filled in*).

I understand that failure without lawful excuse to attend court in accordance with this promise to appear is an offence under subsection 133(5) of the *Criminal Code*.

Subsections 133(5) and (6) of the *Criminal Code* state as follows:

(5) Promise to Appear (Police) and requirement to attend for prints and photos

"(5) Every one who is named in an appearance notice or promise to appear, or in a recognizance entered into before an officer in charge, that has been confirmed by a justice under section 455.4 and who fails, without lawful excuse, the proof of which lies upon him, to attend court in accordance therewith, is guilty of
    (a) an indictable offence and is liable to imprisonment for two years, or
    (b) an offence punishable on summary conviction.
(6) For the purposes of subsection (5), it is not a lawful excuse that an appearance notice, promise to appear or recognizance states defectively the substance of the alleged offence."

Section 453.4 of the *Criminal Code* states as follows:

"**453.4** Where an accused who is required by an appearance notice or promise to appear or by a recognizance entered into before an officer in charge to appear at a time and place stated therein for the purposes of the *Identification of Criminals Act* does not appear at that time and place, a justice may, where the appearance notice, promise to appear or recognizance has been confirmed by a justice under section 455.4, issue a warrant for the arrest of the accused for the offence with which he is charged."

Dated this .... day of .... A.D. ...., at ....

....
(*Signature of accused*)

R.S., c. 2 (2nd Supp.) s. 23(2).

Appendix D
List of Selected Summary, Hybrid, and Indictable Offences

CRIMINAL CODE

1. Summary Offences

s.171	Causing a disturbance
s.173	Prowl by night
s.193(2)	Inmate of a common bawdy house
s.195.1	Offences in relation to prostitution Communicating, etcetera
s.295	Take auto without consent
s.330(2)	Indecent phone calls
(3)	Harrassing phone calls
s.401	Injuring or endangering animals
s.402	Cruelty to animals
s.412	Possession of slugs

2. Hybrid or Dual Procedure Offences (maximum sentence for an adult if proceeded by indictment is indicated).

s.84	Point a firearm — 5 years
	Careless use of firearm — 2 years
s.87	Carry concealed weapon — 5 years
s.88	Possession of a prohibited weapon — 5 years
s.118	Obstructing police — 2 years
s.128	Public Mischief — 5 years
s.133(1)	Escape custody, unlawfully at large — 2 years
s.133(2)	Fail to appear in court — 2 years
s.133(3)	Fail to comply with conditions of release — 2 years
s.233(1)	Dangerous driving — 5 years
s.236	Fail to remain — 2 years
s.239	Impaired/Over 80, driving — 5 years
s.245	Assault — 5 years
s.246	Assault police — 5 years
s.246.1	Sexual assault — 10 years
s.294	Theft under $1000. — 2 years
s.301.1	Credit card offences — 10 years
s.313	Possession of stolen property under $1000. — 2 years
s.320(2)	False pretences under $1000. — 2 years
s.387(3)	Mischief to property — over $1000. — 10 years
(4)	— under $1000. — 2 years
s.393	False fire alarm — 2 years

3. **Straight Indictable Offences (maximum sentence for an adult is indicated).**

s.80	Possession of explosive substances — 5 years
s.85	Possession of dangerous weapon — 10 years
s.121	Perjury — 14 years
s.125	Fabricating evidence — 14 years
s.127(2)	Attempting to obstruct justice — 10 years
s.176	Common nuisance — 2 years
s.218-19	Manslaughter, 1st & 2nd degree murder — life imprisonment
s.233(3)	Dangerous driving causing bodily harm — 10 years
s.233(4)	Dangerous driving causing death — 14 years
s.239(2)	Impaired/Over 80 driving causing bodily harm — 10 years
s.239(3)	Impaired/Over 80 driving causing death — 14 years
s.243.4(2)	Uttering threats re: death or bodily harm — 5 years
s.245.1	Assault with weapon or causing bodily harm — 10 years
s.245.2	Aggravated assault — 14 years
s.246.2	Sexual assault with a weapon — 14 years
s.246.3	Aggravated sexual assault — life imprisonment
s.294	Theft over $1000. — 10 years
s.303	Robbery — life imprisonment
s.305	Extortion — life imprisonment
s.306	Break and enter dwelling house — life imprisonment
	Break and enter other place — 14 years
s.309(1)	Possession of house breaking instruments — 10 years
s.313	Possession of property obtained by crime over $1000. — 10 years
s.314	Theft from the mails — 10 years
s.320(2)	False pretences over $1000. — 10 years
s.325	Forgery — 14 years
s.326	Uttering a forged document — 14 years
s.330(1)	False messages — 2 years
s.389(1)	Arson — 14 years
s.390	Set fire to other substance — 5 years
s.392	Set fire by negligence — 5 years

NARCOTIC CONTROL ACT

1. **Hybrid or Dual Procedure Offence**
s.3   Possession of a narcotic — maximum sentence for an adult if proceeded by indictment is 7 years

2. **Straight Indictable Offence**
s.4   Possession for the purpose of trafficking or trafficking in a narcotic — Maximum sentence for an adult is life imprisonment.

Endnotes

These notes are provided for those who wish to refer to a specific point or section in the *Young Offenders Act, Criminal Code,* and *Canadian Charter of Rights and Freedoms.*

Page	Line	Note
20	1	*Young Offenders Act*, s.4
20	38	*Young Offenders Act*, s.44.1-44.2
21	4	*Young Offenders Act*, s.44.2(2)
21	7	*Young Offenders Act*, s.38
21	16	*Young Offenders Act*, s.38(1.2)
21	20	*Criminal Code*, s.450(2) and 451
21	33	*Criminal Code*, s.449
22	18	*Criminal Code*, s.450
22	25	*Canadian Charter of Rights and Freedoms*, s.10: "Everyone has the right on arrest or detention; (a) to be informed promptly of the reasons therefore; (b) to retain and instruct counsel without delay and to be informed of that right..."
22	27	*Young Offenders Act*, s.3(e) and s.11(2)
22	39	*Young Offenders Act*, s.56
23	7	*Young Offenders Act*, s.38
23	10	*Young Offenders Act*, s.7
23	13	*Young Offenders Act*, s.9(1), (2)
23	20	*Canadian Charter of Rights and Freedoms*, s.24(2): "Where... a court concludes that evidence was obtained in a manner that infringed or denied any rights or freedoms guaranteed by this Charter, the evidence shall be excluded if it is established that... the admission of it in the proceedings would bring the administration of justice into disrepute."
23	24	*Young Offenders Act*, s.56(4), (5)
23	27	*Young Offenders Act*, s.9(8), (9), (10)
23	32	*Criminal Code*, s.246, assault police; s.118, obstruct police
23	39	*Young Offenders Act*, s.9(2)
24	2	*Young Offenders Act*, s.9(1)
24	4	*Young Offenders Act*, s.56
24	18	*Young Offenders Act*, s.44
24	32	*Young Offenders Act*, s.45
24	39	*Criminal Code*, s.133(4), (5), (8)
25	6	*Criminal Code*, s.450-453.1
25	23	*Criminal Code*, s.452-453.1
25	35	*Young Offenders Act*, s.11
27	29	*Young Offenders Act*, s.6
29	2	*Young Offenders Act*, s.60
29	19	*Criminal Code*, s.120-121
29	28	*Young Offenders Act*, s.11

Page	Line	Note
29	36	*Young Offenders Act*, s.11
30	17	*Young Offenders Act*, s.11(8)
31	28	*Young Offenders Act*, s.12(1) and (2)
31	33	*Young Offenders Act*, s.12(3)
32	35	*Criminal Code*, s.133
33	14	*Young Offenders Act*, s.9
33	21	*Young Offenders Act*, s.10
33	23	*Young Offenders Act*, s.10(3)
34	16	*Young Offenders Act*, s.16(2)
34	38	*Young Offenders Act*, s.13
34	39	*Young Offenders Act*, s.16(3)
35	2	*Young Offenders Act*, s.17
35	16	*Criminal Code*, s.633
36	22	*Young Offenders Act*, s.51
36	26	*Criminal Code*, ss.448-454, 457
36	28	*Young Offenders Act*, s.6
36	32	*Young Offenders Act*, s.8(2)
37	20	*Criminal Code*, s.457(7)
38	22	*Young Offenders Act*, s.38
38	31	*Criminal Code*, s.457.2
40	6	*Young Offenders Act*, s.3(2)
40	7	*Young Offenders Act*, s.7.1
40	13	*Young Offenders Act*, s.7.1(2)
40	17	*Young Offenders Act*, s.7.1(3)
40	26	*Young Offenders Act*, s.7(2)
40	32	*Young Offenders Act*, s.13
41	26	*Criminal Code*, s.133(3)
41	33	*Criminal Code*, s.457.8(2)(c)
41	36	*Criminal Code*, s.457.8(2)(a)
42	34	*Young Offenders Act*, s.48-49
43	3	*Criminal Code*, s.700
43	7	*Criminal Code*, s.703
43	10	*Criminal Code*, s.133(3)
43	28	*Criminal Code*, s.457(5.1)
43	39	*Criminal Code*, s.454
44	4	*Criminal Code*, s.457.1
44	7	*Young Offenders Act*, s.11(2), (3)
44	29	*Young Offenders Act*, s.10
44	36	*Criminal Code*, s.457.3(b)
45	4	*Young Offenders Act*, s.9(1)
45	39	*Criminal Code*, s.133(1)(a)
48	15	*Young Offenders Act*, s.52
48	24	*Young Offenders Act*, s.38
48	33	*Young Offenders Act*, s.39
49	6	*Young Offenders Act*, s.11
49	21	*Young Offenders Act*, s.27(2)
51	25	*Criminal Code*, s.457.8(1)(b)(ii)
51	27	*Criminal Code*, s.457.8(2)(a)

Page	Line	Note
52	18	*Young Offenders Act*, s.56(4)
52	35	*Young Offenders Act*, s.13
53	8	*Criminal Code*, s.16
53	36	*Young Offenders Act*, s.27
55	25	*Young Offenders Act*, s.12(1)
55	28	*Young Offenders Act*, s.12(3)
55	30	*Young Offenders Act*, s.12(4)
56	23	*Young Offenders Act*, s.19(1)
56	27	*Young Offenders Act*, s.19(2)
56	29	Chapter Seven and Chapter Eight
56	31	Chapter Four
56	34	*Criminal Code*, s.457.8(1)(b)(ii)
56	39	*Criminal Code*, s.457.8(2)(a)
57	12	*Young Offenders Act*, s.39(3)
58	3	*Criminal Code*, s.594
58	19	*Young Offenders Act*, s.3(c) and (f)
59	13	*Young Offenders Act*, s.14
59	21	*Young Offenders Act*, s.14(2)
59	29	*Young Offenders Act*, s.14(6)
59	32	*Young Offenders Act*, s.24(2)
59	35	*Young Offenders Act*, s.24(3)
60	1	*Young Offenders Act*, s.14(1)
60	15	*Young Offenders Act*
60	19	*Young Offenders Act*, s.13(1)(e)
61	1	*Young Offenders Act*
61	6	*Young Offenders Act*, s.20(7)
61	10	*Young Offenders Act*, s.20(6)
61	15	*Young Offenders Act*, s.20(3)
61	17	Below at pp. 63 and 67-68
61	20	*Young Offenders Act*, s.20(4)
61	34	*Young Offenders Act*, s.20(4.1)
62	3	*Young Offenders Act*, s.20(5)
62	11	*Young Offenders Act*, s.20(1)(a)
62	28	*Young Offenders Act*, s.20(1)(b)
62	32	*Young Offenders Act*, s.21(1)
62	36	*Young Offenders Act*, s.20(8)
62	39	*Young Offenders Act*, s.21(2)
63	1	*Young Offenders Act*, s.20(1)(c)-(f)
63	6	*Young Offenders Act*, s.20(1)(c)
63	12	*Young Offenders Act*, s.20(1)(f)
63	15	*Young Offenders Act*, s.20(1)(d)
63	19	*Young Offenders Act*, s.20(1)(g)
63	26	*Young Offenders Act*, s.21(7)
63	30	*Young Offenders Act*, s.21(8)
63	36	*Young Offenders Act*, s.21(9)
63	38	*Young Offenders Act*, s.20(1)(h)
64	7	*Young Offenders Act*, s.20(1)(i)
64	9	*Young Offenders Act*, s.20(3)

Page	Line	Note
64	12	*Young Offenders Act*, s.22(1), (2)
64	18	*Young Offenders Act*, s.20(1)(j)
64	24	*Young Offenders Act*, s.23(5)
64	25	*Young Offenders Act*, s.23(4)
64	27	*Young Offenders Act*, s.23(1)
65	7	*Young Offenders Act*, s.26
65	12	*Young Offenders Act*, s.23(2)(g)
65	21	*Young Offenders Act*, s.23(2)(f)
65	30	*Young Offenders Act*, s.24
65	34	*Young Offenders Act*, s.20(1)(k)
65	37	*Young Offenders Act*, s.24(3)
66	6	*Young Offenders Act*, s.24(1)
66	15	*Young Offenders Act*, s.24.1
66	18	*Young Offenders Act*, s.24.2(4)
66	20	*Young Offenders Act*, s.35
66	34	*Young Offenders Act*, s.24.1(4)
66	36	*Young Offenders Act*, s.24.1(3)
66	37	*Young Offenders Act*, s.24.4
67	7	*Young Offenders Act*, s.20(7)
67	12	*Criminal Code*, s.722(1)
67	20	*Young Offenders Act*, s.20(1)(k)
67	25	*Young Offenders Act*, s.20(4)
67	32	*Young Offenders Act*, s.20(4.1)
67	38	*Young Offenders Act*, s.24.3
68	14	*Young Offenders Act*, s.24.3(2)
68	16	*Young Offenders Act*, s.24.3(1)
68	23	*Criminal Code*, s.133(1)
68	27	*Young Offenders Act*, s.24.1(3)(b) and s.24.1(4)(c)
68	30	*Young Offenders Act*, s.24.2(9)
68	33	*Young Offenders Act*, s.35
68	38	*Young Offenders Act*, s.20(1)(*l*)
69	15	*Young Offenders Act*, s.26
69	16	*Young Offenders Act*, s.24.1(3)(b) 24.1(4)(c)
73	36	*Young Offenders Act*, s.27
74	19	*Young Offenders Act*
74	22	*Young Offenders Act*, s.11(3)(d)
74	25	*Young Offenders Act*, s.39(3)
74	32	*Young Offenders Act*, s.28(3)
74	34	*Young Offenders Act*, s.28(1)
74	39	*Young Offenders Act*, s.28(17)
75	4	*Young Offenders Act*, s.28(17)
75	15	*Young Offenders Act*, s.29
75	16	*Young Offenders Act*, s.29(4)
75	18	*Young Offenders Act*, ss.30 and 31
75	21	*Young Offenders Act*, s.30(1)
75	26	*Young Offenders Act*, s.31

Page	Line	Note
75	29	*Young Offenders Act*, s.30(6)
75	32	*Young Offenders Act*, s.32
75	35	*Young Offenders Act*, s.32(1)
76	1	*Young Offenders Act*, s.32(2)
76	7	*Young Offenders Act*, s.32(7), (8)
76	10	*Young Offenders Act*, s.21(10)
77	16	*Young Offenders Act*, s.45(1)(a)
77	18	*Young Offenders Act*, ss.40-46
77	21	*Young Offenders Act*, ss.44.1, 44.2
77	37	*Young Offenders Act*, s.45(1)(e), (f)
78	1	*Young Offenders Act*, s.45(2)
78	3	*Young Offenders Act*, s.45(4)
78	6	*Young Offenders Act*, s.45.1-45.2
78	17	*Young Offenders Act*, s.50
78	28	*Criminal Code*, ss.21-23.1
78	36	*Young Offenders Act*, s.14(2)(b)
79	5	*Young Offenders Act*, s.20(1)(c)
79	6	*Young Offenders Act*, s.20(1)(f) and s.21(6)
79	12	*Young Offenders Act*, s.20(1)(d)
79	19	*Young Offenders Act*, s.39(1)
79	23	*Young Offenders Act*, s.38(1)
79	25	*Young Offenders Act*, s.38(1.4)

Printed in Canada